MISSISSIPPI

AN ILLUSTRATED GUIDE TO THE

MODERN

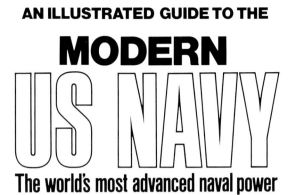

US NAVY

The world's most advanced naval power

An Arco Military Book

Published by
PRENTICE HALL PRESS
New York

AN ILLUSTRATED GUIDE TO THE

MODERN

US NAVY

The world's most advanced naval power
John Jordan

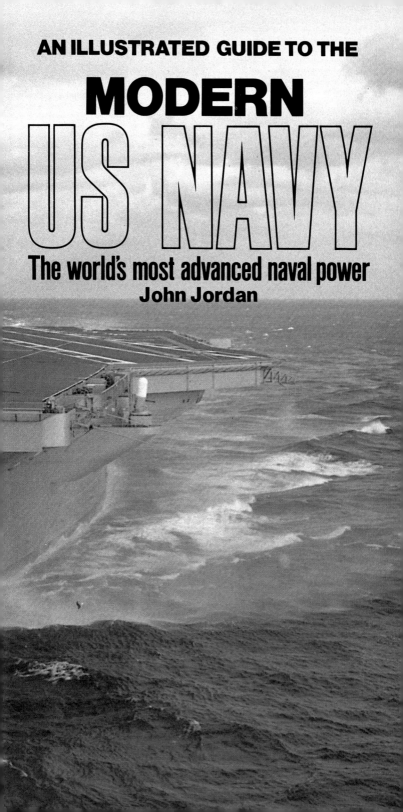

A Salamander Book

An Arco Military Book

Published by Prentice Hall Press,
A Division of Simon & Schuster, Inc.
Simon & Schuster Building
Rockefeller Center
1230 Avenue of the Americas
New York, New York 10020

PRENTICE HALL PRESS is a
trademark of Simon & Schuster, Inc.

1 2 3 4 5 6 7 8 9 10

Library of Congress Catalog Card
Number 81 71937

ISBN 0-668-05505-7

This book may not be sold outside
the USA and Canada.

Contents

Vessels are arranged within sections of classes, and are listed under the name ship of that
class. Classification initials are given at the beginning of each entry, and are explained in
a table on page 10.

Credits

Author: John Jordan is a contributor to many important defense journals, a consultant to the Soviet section of 1980-81 "Jane's Fighting Ships", co-author of Salamander's "Balance of Military Power", and has written a companion "Guide", concerned with the modern US Navy

Editor: Ray Bonds
Designer: Barry Savage

Photographs: All official US Navy photographs supplied by Navy Department, US Department of Defense, Washington, DC.
Line drawings: ©John Jordan.
Diagrams: TIGA©Salamander Books Ltd.
Filmset: Modern Text Typesetting Ltd.
Color reproduction by Rodney Howe Ltd.
Printed in Belgium by Henri Proost et Cie.

Development of the US Navy

The geographical situation of the United States, separated from Europe by the Atlantic and from the mainland of Asia by the even broader expanses of the Pacific, makes the possession of a strong navy imperative. The United States Navy is the primary instrument for the projection of American military power and political influence into these distant regions, and it is at the same time the means by which the United States maintains control over the seas in order to ensure the security of its maritime communications and of its territory in the event of hostilities with another power.

These twin missions of power projection and sea control cannot be considered in total isolation from one another. In order to project power against a distant land mass a navy must be able to exercise control over the seas which its forces will have to transit in order to reach their objective and over the operating area from which the air strikes and amphibious assault will be made. Similarly, the job of exercising sea control over broad ocean areas is made much easier if forward-deployed power projection forces compel the enemy to adopt a defensive posture. The power projection and sea control missions should therefore be seen as two sides of the same coin. The problem is that of finding the right balance between those forces required for "offensive"—ie, power projection—missions and those required for "defensive"—ie, sea control—missions.

In time of war, when funds and resources are virtually unlimited, there is no conflict of interests; a country the size of the United

Note: This Guide deals with surface vessels of the US Navy; submarines of the US Navy (and others) are covered in a companion volume, *An Illustrated Guide to Modern Submarines*.

US Fleet Organisation

The basic units of organisation for the purposes of deployment are as follows: —

Carrier Battle Group

Centred around a single carrier (CV), this generally includes an escort group of four to six ships. The typical composition of such a group would be:

1 or 2 CGs armed with Terrier
1 DDG armed with Tartar
2 or 3 ASW destroyers (DD) or frigates (FF)

Nuclear-powered carriers (CVN) are usually deployed with a homogeneous group of nuclear-powered escorts (CGN).

Amphibious Squadron (PhibRon)

Composed of between three and five amphibious vessels and two escorts (FF/FFG). The typical composition of a PhibRon would be:

1 LPH
1 LPD, 1 LSD
2 LST

A PhibRon based on an LHA would omit the LPH and LSD.

Before the crisis in the Arabian Gulf US Navy deployments were maintained on the following pattern:

Forward Deployed Forces

Pacific Fleet

Third Fleet	**Seventh Fleet** (NW Pacific, SE Asia)
4 Carrier Battle Groups 2 PhibRons	2 Carrier Battle Groups 2 PhibRons

Atlantic Fleet

US Naval Forces Europe

Second Fleet	**Sixth Fleet** (Mediterranean)	**Middle East Force**
4 Carrier Battle Groups 3 PhibRons	2 Carrier Battle Groups 1 PhibRon	1 flagship (AGF) 2 FF

Since late 1979, however, one of the Seventh Fleet and one of the Sixth Fleet Carrier Battle Groups have been deployed to the Indian Ocean on a regular basis. They have been reinforced by one of the Seventh Fleet PhibRons.

Left: Six US Navy nuclear-powered cruisers operating together in exercise READEX 1-81. The force comprises the four ships of the Virginia class and both ships of the California class.

States simply builds what it needs. In peacetime, however, the inevitable constraints on the defence budget mean that difficult choices have to be made; more of one type of ship means less of another. Factions supporting a particular aspect of naval operations—the aviators, the submariners, the surface ship lobby—begin to dig their heels in, and bitter conflicts break out over the crucial issue of what sort of forces the navy should have, and in what numbers. It is against this background that the development of the US Navy over the past three decades must be seen.

The 1950s

The advent of the atomic bomb threw American naval strategy in the immediate postwar period into a state of total confusion.

Many questioned the survivability of any sort of task force in the face of the new weaponry. In 1950, however, came a new conflict, which served to emphasise once again the value of traditional power projection forces. The Korean War re-established the aircraft carrier and the amphibious assault force as the twin central elements of American sea-power, and set off a massive naval reconstruction programme. Between 1955 and 1962 no fewer than seven super-carriers—one of which was nuclear-powered—were completed.

In addition to the standard light attack squadrons, they would be able to operate strategic bombers (A—3 Skywarriors) which could launch nuclear strikes deep into the heart of the Soviet Union. The

primary mission of the large numbers of war-built surface units—destroyers and cruisers—would continue to be the protection of the carriers, with a subsidiary fire-support role in amphibious operations.

Although the development of both surface-to-surface and surface-to-air missiles proceeded simultaneously throughout the 1950s, submarine- and ship-launched SSMs did not find favour in the US Navy in the way that they did in the Soviet Navy because of the renewed confidence in carrier-borne aviation.

Below: The Vietnam war reinforced the bias of the US Navy towards the power projection mission. Here an A-7 Corsair attack aircraft is lined up on one of the forward catapults of a carrier.

Surface-to-air missiles, on the other hand, received massive development funds because of their potential value in defence of the carrier task force, and an entire "family" of missiles—Talos, Terrier and Tartar—was in service aboard a variety of US ships by the early 1960s.

The first missile ships were converted war-built cruisers (CAGs and CLGs) but, with the tailing-off of the carrier programme, funds became available for three classes each of ten "frigates" (DLGs) armed with the Terrier long-range missile, and a large class of destroyers (DDGs) armed with the medium-range Tartar. A programme for the development of the even more capable—and costly—Typhoon missile was set in motion. (This particular project was to founder but was later revived as Aegis.).

In the 1950s the threat to US sea control was minimal. The Soviet Navy, although growing rapidly in size, was still little more than a coast defence force. The air strikes and amphibious assaults of the Korean War had been unopposed. The only US ships specifically built for the sea control mission in this period were a handful of diesel-powered destroyer escorts (DEs), which were not much of an improvement on their war-built counterparts.

Only in the NATO Eastlant area, which was threatened by a growing Soviet submarine fleet based on the Kola Peninsula, was sea control thought to merit any serious attention, and a number of war-built Essex-class carriers were modified as ASW carriers (CVSs) carrying S-2 Tracker aircraft and HSS-1 helicopters. They would form the centre of submarine hunter-killer groups and convoy escort groups. As far as possible the sea control mission in the European Theatre would be devolved onto the NATO navies, which were boosted by American construction and American finance under the Mutual Defense Aid Program (MDAP).

US Navy Classification System

Note:
In June 1975 a new system of classification was adopted. Vessels formerly classified as "Frigates" (DLG/DLGN) became "Cruisers" (CG/CGN), and "Destroyer Escorts" (DE/DEG) became "Frigates" (FF/FFG).

CVN (ex-CVAN)	nuclear-powered aircraft carrier
CV (ex-CVA)	aircraft carrier
CGN (ex-CLGN/DLGN)	nuclear-powered missile cruiser
CG (ex-DLGN)	missile cruiser
DDG	missile destroyer (AAW)
DD	destroyer (ASW)
FFG (ex-DEG)	missile frigate (AAW)
FF (ex-DE)	frigate (ASW)
PHM	missile patrol hydrofoil
LCC	amphibious command ship
LHA	amphibious assault ship (multi-purpose)
LPH	amphibious assault ship
LPD	amphibious transport dock
LSD	dock landing ship
LST	tank landing ship
AD	destroyer tender
AS	submarine tender
AE	ammunition ship
AFS	combat support ship
AO	oiler
AOE	fast combat support ship
AOR	replenishment oiler

The classification system used by the US Navy is frequently extended—often incorrectly—to ships of other navies. Note the distinction between the suffix "G" (=surface-to-air) and the suffix "M" (=antiship) used for missile ships.

1960s—More of the same

From 1960 onwards the mission of nuclear strike on the Soviet Union was transferred from the big carriers to the Polaris submarine. No sooner was the latter programme under way, however, than the value of conventional power projection forces in a limited conflict was reaffirmed by American involvement in the Vietnam War.

For nearly a decade the big carriers conducted sustained strike operations against targets in North Vietnam and in support of friendly forces in the South. Studies were undertaken for new classes of nuclear-powered carriers (CVANs) and nuclear-powered missile escorts (DLGNs), and a massive programme of amphibious construction—some 60 vessels in all—was instituted to replace the aging force of war-built vessels.

The escort problem

While attention was focused yet again on the construction of ever more capable—and costly— power projection units, the forces of sea control continued to be neglected. Many of the war-built destroyers underwent extensive FRAM (Fleet Rehabilitation And Modernisation) refits in the early 1960s to equip them with ASROC, new sonars, and DASH (Drone Anti-Submarine Helicopters), and these now became the workhorses of the sea control mission. But the only new vessels completed during the 1960s were a handful of "convoy escorts" (DEs), begin-

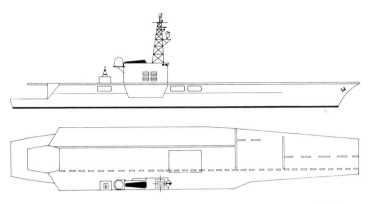

Above: Profile and plan views of the Sea Control Ship (SCS) proposed in the early 1970s by Admiral Zumwalt.

ning with the two prototypes of the Bronstein class.

The new ships, which aimed to avoid the high costs increasingly associated with fleet escorts while providing a first-class ASW capability which would enable them to deal effectively with the new generation of fast, nuclear-powered Soviet submarines, were designed on traditional American "all-or-nothing" principles. They were fitted with the most advanced anti-submarine weapons and sensors: the massive SQS-26 bow sonar, ASROC and DASH. The "platform" characteristics, on the other hand, were distinctly second-rate, with only a single screw and a maximum speed of only 25 to 27kts. AAW capabilities were minimal except in the Brooke class, which proved too expensive for construction beyond six units.

In the mid-1960s, with block obsolescence looming for the large number of war-built destroyers, orders began to be placed for the 46-strong Knox class. But the new escorts were not popular with some factions in the naval community; concern was expressed about the limited military capabilities of the ships and about their one-shaft propulsion plant. The next escort design, the DDX, which began as an attempt to provide a simple ASW destroyer for fleet work, resulted in the controversial

Spruance class, which came out at 8,000 tons—three times the displacement of the war-built destroyers they were to replace—and were the ultimate in sophistication.

By 1970 the only designs on the drawing board were sophisticated power projection types: the Nimitz-class CVANs, the Tarawa-class LHAs, the Virginia-class DLGNs, the Spruance-class DDs and the Los Angeles-class SSNs (all three of the last-named types designed primarily for fleet work in support of the carrier battle groups).

Zumwalt and Project 60

Such was the situation that confronted Admiral Elmo Zumwalt when he became Chief of Naval Operations in 1970. Unlike his three predecessors, who were all aviators, Zumwalt was a surface navy man, and he immediately set about changing what he regarded as an alarming imbalance in the Navy's construction programme. Zumwalt felt that American naval commitment in South Asia over the previous two decades had distorted the strategic picture in favour of projection forces and that the growing threat posed by the Soviet Navy to American control of the seas in the event of war between NATO and the forces of the Warsaw Pact had been seriously neglected. The war-built destroyers and the

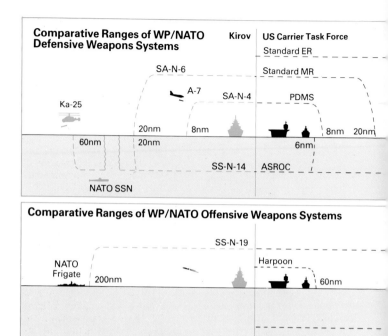

Comparative Ranges of WP/NATO Defensive Weapons Systems

Kirov | US Carrier Task Force

Standard ER

SA-N-6 | Standard MR

A-7 | SA-N-4 | PDMS

Ka-25

20nm | 8nm | 8nm | 20nm

60nm | 20nm | 6nm

SS-N-14 | ASROC

NATO SSN

Comparative Ranges of WP/NATO Offensive Weapons Systems

SS-N-19

NATO Frigate | Harpoon

200nm | 60nm

Above: A comparison of the offensive and defensive capabilities of a US carrier battle group (CBG) with those of a Soviet surface action group centred on the cruiser *Kirov* reveals why the US Navy is so reluctant to abandon the large-deck carrier.

Below: A carrier battle group (CBG) centred on the carrier *Midway* (CV-41) operating in the Indian Ocean.

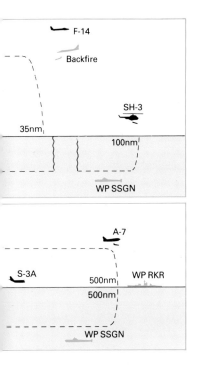

Essex-class CVs on which the Navy still largely depended to perform the sea control mission were by now 25 years old, yet even with the 30-strong Spruance class the US Navy would possess only 180 out of the 250 escorts which it regarded as the minimum figure required to perform its missions. The US Navy needed large numbers of new hulls, and quickly.

Zumwalt elevated his own "High-Low" concept to the level of a philosophy. The "high" end of the Navy would be the high-performance ships and weapon systems needed to perform the projection mission in high-threat areas. The "low" end would consist of moderate-performance ships which, because of their low cost, could be produced in large numbers for the sea control mission.

Within 60 days of his accession Zumwalt produced Project 60, which was to form the basis for major changes in the Navy's construction policy during the 1970s. The "high" programme was already in full swing, and the only modification made to it was the cancellation of the last four of nine projected LHAs.

But it was now to be balanced by a "low" programme financed in part by the premature retirement of large numbers of war-built ships and based on four new classes. Of these the most important were the Patrol Frigate (PF) and the Sea Control Ship (SCS). The PF, which became the FFG 7 class, was a development of the convoy escort types built during the 1960s, but with enhanced AAW and anti-surface capabilities in order to counter the new Soviet long-range maritime bombers and forward deployment of surface units.

The SCS was an austere ASW carrier designed to operate 14 SH-3 ASW helicopters and three AV-8A Harrier V/STOL aircraft. The SCS was affordable in large numbers—eight could be purchased for the price of one CVAN—and was the obvious replacement for the CVSs of the Essex class. Zumwalt went further and suggested that in peacetime the SCSs would take the place of the big carriers on forward deployments in order to blunt the threat posed by Soviet surface action groups (SAGs), and that the big carriers would be held back in low-threat areas until hostilities began, when they would exchange places with the SCSs.

Other important related projects were the acceleration of the LAMPS manned helicopter programme in order to increase the number of air-capable platforms, and of the development of the Harpoon SSM, which would spread offensive capabilities throughout the fleet instead of leaving them concentrated on the decks of a handful of strike carriers.

In order to provide the necessary coordination for these various weapons platforms Zumwalt initiated the development of a network of satellite-based communication and surveillance systems.

Above: The battleship *New Jersey* (BB-62) is to be reactivated and armed with Harpoon and Tomahawk missiles.

Below: US design philosophy favours sophisticated multi-function weapons systems and radars whereas the Soviet Navy favours larger numbers of single-purpose systems. The Soviet Kara (above) and USS *Virginia* (below) illustrate this contrast.

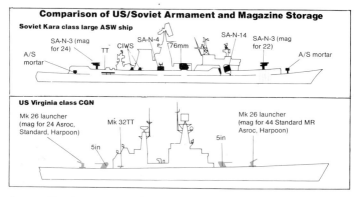

Comparison of US/Soviet Armament and Magazine Storage

Soviet Kara class large ASW ship

A/S mortar — SA-N-3 (mag for 24) — TT — CIWS — SA-N-4 — 76mm — SA-N-14 — SA-N-3 (mag for 22) — A/S mortar

US Virginia class CGN

Mk 26 launcher (mag for 24 Asroc, Standard, Harpoon) — 5in — Mk 32TT — 5in — Mk 26 launcher (mag for 44 Standard MR Asroc, Harpoon)

A continuing struggle

When Zumwalt retired as CNO in 1974, the battle between the power projection and sea control factions resumed in earnest. The first victim of the new battle was the Sea Control Ship, which, following evaluation trials employing the LPH *Guam*, was declared to be unable to defend itself against the growing threat from Soviet long-range bombers.

The real reason for its demise, however, was undoubtedly the fear of the aviators that the project would reduce the funds available for attack carrier con-struction and for the purchase of carrier aircraft, and that by taking the place of the big carriers in the "front line" in peacetime the SCS would seriously reduce their credibility—and consequently the willingness of Congress to continue to provide virtually un-limited funds to maintain force levels.

The aviators were, however, compelled to make one signifi-cant concession. From 1975 the big carriers ceased to be designa-ted Attack Carriers (CVA); instead they become "Multi-Mission" Carriers (CV) and accep-

ted squadrons of S-3A Viking ASW aircraft and SH-3H Sea King ASW helicopters in place of some of their strike aircraft. This modification equipped them to provide more effective distant cover for convoys and to perform more general sub-hunting operations, using data from the SOSUS seabed surveillance system. it also provided an increasingly necessary long-range ASW defence capability to a battle group faced by growing numbers of submarines armed with cruise missiles.

Harpoon and Tomahawk

By the late 1970s large numbers of the Navy's ships had been fitted with the Harpoon SSM and there was the prospect of a follow-on, Tomahawk, with a range comparable to that of the largest cruise missiles in service with the Soviet Navy. The development of long-range cruise missiles, however, has inevitably led to increased polarisation of the aviation and surface ship camps. Long-range cruise missiles in a maritime environment need an extensive—and costly—satellite-based Extended Horizon Command and Control (EHC) system on the Soviet pattern. They would also be most effective if used in conjunction with VTOL aircraft scattered among a number of surface warships.

Proposals such as these have attracted considerable criticism from the aviation lobby, who have pointed out that distributing aircraft among a variety of small hulls is uneconomic in terms of ship space and maintenance facilities. Supporters of the big carriers claim, with some justification, that the carrier battle group is still the most capable, versatile and cost-effective strike weapon available, and that to adopt an essentially "defensive" sea control posture is to play into the hands of the Soviet Navy.

Present and future

The dramatic increase in defence spending proposed by the Reagan Administration in its first year of office has served to ease—temporarily, at least—some of these conflicts. Under an increased budget there is no reason why the construction of high-value super-carriers and their large, sophisticated escorts should not go hand in hand with a large programme of cheap frigates and the widespread fitting of Tomahawk missiles.

With the application of additional resources, however, thinking has grown more conservative. There have been proposals to drag some of the older carriers, and even the four Iowa-class battleships, out of retirement in order to re-establish mastery over the seas, while new technology programmes such as the Surface Effect Ship (SES) have foundered without trace.

A 600-ship Navy is planned instead of the present total of 450. There are strong indications, however, that the US budget is in trouble and will not be able to sustain this level of expansion. In the Navy's case the problem will be exacerbated by manning difficulties and the additional strain on its resources imposed by new commitments in the Indian Ocean. It therefore appears inevitable that before long the battle between the advocates of power projection and sea control forces will be renewed with even greater intensity.

Aircraft Carriers

Nimitz

Completed: 1975 onwards.
Names: CVN 68 *Nimitz;* CVN 69 *Dwight D. Eisenhower;* CVN 70 *Carl Vinson,* CVN 71 *Theodore Roosevelt.* (building).
Displacement: 81,600t standard; 91,400t full load.
Dimensions: 1,092 oa x 134 wl, 251 flight deck x 37ft (332.8 x 40.8, 76.4 x 11.3m).
Propulsion: 4-shaft nuclear; 2 A4W reactors; 260,000shp = 30kts.
Armament: *AAW:* 3 BPDMS launchers Mk 25 (3x8).
Aircraft: 24 F-14A Tomcat; 24 A-7E Corsair; 10-A6E Intruder + 4 KA-6D; 4 E-2C Hawkeye; 4 EA-6B Prowler; 10 S-3A Viking; 6 SH-3H Sea King.
Sensors: *Surveillance:* SPS-48, SPS-43A, SPS-10. *Fire Control:* 3 Mk 115.

The large aircraft carrier remains the "capital ship" of the US Navy. At present twelve carriers, each serving at the centre of a Carrier Battle Group (CBG), are maintained in the active fleet, while a thirteenth ship—at present Saratoga (CV-60)—undergoes a major modernisation as part of the Service Life Extension Programme. All except the older Midway class carriers (to be replaced by two new CVNs) now operate squadrons of ASW aircraft in addition to their attack and fighter squadrons.

The Nimitz class was originally envisaged as a replacement for the three Midway-class carriers. The completion of the first nuclear-powered carrier, *Enterprise*, had been followed by the construction of two conventionally powered ships, *America* and *John F. Kennedy*. The latter had, however, only ever been thought of as "interim" designs to plug the gap between *Enterprise* and a second generation of nuclear carriers which would employ smaller numbers of more advanced reactors to provide the necessary power, and which would, it was hoped, cost less to build. The two A4W reactors which power the Nimitz class each produce approximately 130,000shp compared with only 35,000shp for each of the eight A2W reactors aboard *Enterprise*. Moreover, the uranium cores need replacing far less frequently than those originally used in *Enterprise*, giving a full 13-year period between refuellings.

The reduction in the number of reactors from eight to two allowed for major improvements in the internal arrangements below hangar-deck level. ▶

Below: A carrier of the Nimitz class underway. Note the massive "hurricane" bow and the overhang of the angled deck.

▶Whereas in *Enterprise* the entire centre section of the ship is occupied by the machinery rooms, with the aviation fuel compartments and munitions magazines pushed out towards the ends of the ship, in *Nimitz* the propulsion machinery is dvided into two separate units, with the magazines between them and forward of them. The improved arrangement has resulted in an increase of 20 per cent in aviation fuel capacity and a similar increase in the volume available for munitions and stores.

Flight-deck layout is almost identical to that of *John F. Kennedy*. At hangar-deck level, however, there has been a significant increase in the provision of maintenance workshops and spare parts stowage. Maintenance shops have all but taken over the large sponson which supports the flight deck, and at the after end of the hangar there is a large bay for aero-engine maintenance and testing. The increased competition for internal volume even in a ship of this size is illustrated by the need to accommodate a total complement of almost 6,300 men, compared with only 4,900 for *Enterprise*—the original *Forrestal* design on which both ships are based provided for 3,800!

Sensor provision and defensive weapons are on a par with *John F. Kennedy*. The SPS-33/34 "billboard" radars fitted to *Enterprise* and the cruiser *Long Beach* proved to be a maintenance nightmare, and *Nimitz* has been provided with conventional rotating 3-D and air search models. The position of the SPS-48 and SPS-43 antennae is reversed in comparison with *John F. Kennedy*. *Nimitz* and *Eisenhower* are scheduled to be fitted with an ▶

Right: *Eisenhower* (CVN-69), showing her vast expanse of flight deck. Two SH-3 Sea King helicopters can be seen on the port side, with a single A-7 Corsair to starboard.

Below: *Nimitz* (CVN-68) during underway replenishment operations. The lifts are in the lowered position to receive stores. Aircraft on deck include the F-4, A-6 and E-2C.

▶ ASW Control Centre and specialised maintenance facilities for the S-3 Viking anti-submarine aircraft; these features were incorporated into *Carl Vinson* while building. The fourth ship of the class may receive the fixed SPY-1A planar antennae associated with Aegis.

Three Mk 25 BPDMS launchers are fitted at present, but these will shortly be replaced by the Mk 29 launcher for NATO Sea Sparrow (IPDMS). This class is also scheduled to receive three Phalanx CIWS guns.

Problems were experienced from the outset in the construction of these ships. *Nimitz* was four years late in commissioning and took seven years to build (*Enterprise* took only four). Her construction was plagued by a shortage of skilled labour and frequent strikes at the Newport News Shipyard. When she was finally completed in 1973, vital components for the A4W reactors had still not been delivered, and a further two years were to elapse before commissioning. This delayed the start of *Eisenhower* by a further four years, and produced a knock-on effect which resulted in

rocketing costs. President Carter attempted, unsuccessfully, to block the authorisation of funds for the construction of a fourth carrier in favour of the smaller, less capable, but less costly CVV design. The CVV, however, was never popular with the Navy, and the Reagan administration has now committed itself to the continuation of the CVN programme.

Both *Nimitz* and *Eisenhower* serve in the Atlantic, and besides the customary deployment to the Mediterranean they have recently seen service in the Indian Ocean.

Below left: The Air Traffic Control Centre of *Eisenhower*.

Bottom: *Eisenhower* (CVN-69) in company with the replenishment oiler *Kalamazoo* (ACR-6) and the destroyer *Coontz* (DDG-40).

Below: *Nimitz* (CVN-68) operating in the Mediterranean.

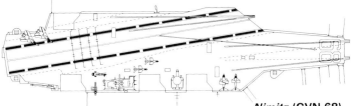

Nimitz (CVN-68).

CVN

Enterprise

Completed: 1961
Name: CVN 65 *Enterprise*
Displacement: 75,700t standard; 89,600t full load.
Dimensions: 1,123 oa x 133 wl, 248 flight deck x 36ft (342.3 x 40.5, 75.7 x 10.9m).
Propulsion: 4-shaft nuclear; 8 A2W reactors; 280,000shp = 30kts.
Armament: 3 NATO Sea Sparrow launchers Mk 29 (3x8); 3 Phalanx CIWS (3x6).
Aircraft: 24 F-14A Tomcat; 24 A-7E Corsair; 10 A-6E Intruder + 4 KA-6D; 4 E-2C Hawkeye; 4 EA-6B Prowler; 10 S-3A Viking; 6 SH-3H Sea King.
Sensors: *Surveillance:* SPS-48C, SPS-49, SPS-65.
Fire Control: 3 Mk 91.

Laid down shortly after the US Navy's first nuclear-powered surface ship, the cruiser *Long Beach, Enterprise* was completed in the remarkably short space of 3 years 9 months. The initial development work on her propulsion plant had begun as early as 1950, and the design of the reactors had benefited from the evaluation of early models installed in submarines. Even so, the problem of producing the required 280,000shp on four shafts employing first-generation reactors resulted in a solution that was costly in terms of internal volume; two A2W reactors are coupled to each shaft and the entire centre section of the ship is taken up by machinery.

Enterprise was also costly in terms of the initial purchase price—nearly double that of her conventionally-powered contemporaries of the Kitty Hawk class—but a number of strong arguments were advanced in favour of nuclear power. Reduced life-cycle costs due to infrequent refuellings made the nuclear-powered carrier a more economic proposition in the longer term, and the CVAN would be capable of undertaking lengthy transits and operations in high-threat areas at a high sustained speed. Moreover, the elimination of ship's fuel bunkers in *Enterprise* allowed a 50 per cent increase in aviation fuel capacity, and consequently in the number of consecutive days of strike operations she could sustain.   ▶

Below left: Stern view of *Enterprise* (CVN-65). Note the overhang of the flight deck to port and to starboard.

Below: *Enterprise* in the late 1970s. She was the first US Navy carrier to operate the F-14 Tomcat, of which six can be seen on the after part of the flight deck.

▶ In size and general layout *Enterprise* is similar to *Kitty Hawk*. The most significant difference as completed was in the shape of the island, which comprised a "box" structure on which were mounted SPS-32/33 "billboard" radars, surmounted by a large cone for ECM and ESM antennae. The SPS-32/33 radars proved difficult to maintain, however, and when *Enterprise* was refitted in 1979-81, the entire island was removed and replaced by a more conventional structure similar to that of the *Nimitz*. As refitted, she will carry conventional rotating radars of the latest types.

Like the carriers of the Kitty Hawk class *Enterprise* was to have received two Mk 10 launchers for Terrier missiles. She was completed with the large sponsons aft, but Terrier was not installed initially in a bid to keep down costs. When Terrier lost favour as a carrier weapon in the mid-1960s, it was decided instead to fit two BPDMS Sea Sparrow launchers on the after sponsons. After her current refit *Enterprise* will carry three Mk 29 launchers for NATO Sea Sparrow, and three Phalanx CIWS guns.

Enterprise began her operational life in the Atlantic, but was transferred together with her nuclear-powered escort group to the Pacific during the Vietnam War and has remained there ever since. A second ship of the class was to have been authorised in the early 1960s but the project was deferred on grounds of cost (see *John F. Kennedy*).

Right: *Enterprise* (CVN-65) underway in the Pacific. In this view she is still operating the F-4 Phantom.

Below: *Enterprise* in company with *Ranger* (CV-61). In her current refit the superstructure will be completely rebuilt.

Kitty Hawk

Completed: 1961-8.
Names: CV63 *Kitty Hawk;* CV64 *Constellation;* CV 66 *America;*
CV 67 *John F. Kennedy.*
Displacement: 60,100-61,000t standard; 80,800-82,000t full load.
Dimensions: 1,048-1,073 oa × 130 wl, 250-268 flight deck × 36ft.
(319.3-326.9 × 39.6, 76.2-81.5 × 11m).
Propulsion: 4-shaft geared steam turbines; 280,000shp = 30kts.
Armament: 2 NATO Sea Sparrow launchers Mk29 (2x8);
CV 64: 2 twin Mk 10 launchers (40 + 40)
for Terrier missiles;
CV 66-7: 3 BPDMS launchers Mk 25 (3x8),
3 Phalanx CIWS.
Aircraft: 24 F-14A Tomcat; 24 A-7E Corsair;
10 A-6E Intruder + 4 KA-6D; 4 E-2C Hawkeye;
4 EA-6B Prowler; 10 S-3A Viking; 6 SH-3H Sea King.
Sensors: *Surveillance:* SPS-48C, SPS-49 (SPS-37A in CV 63),
SPS-10, SPS-65 (CV 67 only).
Fire Control: 4 SPG-55A (CV 64), 2 Mk 91 (CV 63),
3 Mk 115 (CV 66-7).
Sonars: SQS-23 (CV 66 only).

Although there are significant differences between the first pair completed and the last two vessels—*John F. Kennedy* is officially considered as a separate single-ship class—these four carriers are generally grouped together because of their common propulsion system and flight-deck layout.

Kitty Hawk and *Constellation* were ordered as improved Forrestals, incorporating a number of important modifications. The flight deck showed a slight increase in area, and the arrangement of the lifts was revised to improve aircraft-handling arrangements. The single port-side lift, which on the Forrestals was located at the forward end of the flight deck—and was therefore unusable during landing operations—was repositioned at the after end of the overhang, outside the line of the angled deck. The respective positions of the centre lift on the starboard side and the island structure were reversed, so that two lifts were available to serve the forward catapults. A further improved feature of the lifts was that they were no longer strictly rectangular, but had an additional angled section at their forward end which enabled longer aircraft to be accommodated. The new arrangement proved so successful that it was adopted by all subsequent US carriers. ▶

Below left: USS *Kitty Hawk* (CV-63), with over 30 aircraft on deck. The SPS-48 3-D radar is visible aft of the island.

Below: *Kitty Hawk* (CV-63) underway in the Pacific. Four E-2C Hawkeye AEW aircraft are parked on the flight deck.

► *Kitty Hawk* and *Constellation* were designed at a time when long-range surface-to-air missiles were just entering service with the US Navy. In place of the eight 5-inch (127mm) guns of the Forrestal class these ships therefore received two Mk 10 launchers for Terrier missiles positioned on sponsons aft just below the level of the flight deck, with their 40-missile magazines behind them. The SPG-55 guidance radars were fitted close to the launchers and on the island, which became far more cluttered than that of the *Forrestal* because of the need to accommodate a much larger outfit of air search and height-finding radars. To help solve this problem a separate tall lattice mast was placed immediately aft of the island. This has carried a

succession of large 3-D radars, beginning with the SPS-8B, subsequently replaced by the SPS-30, and eventually by the planar SPS-48.

America, the third ship of the class, was completed after a gap of four years and therefore incorporated a number of further modifications. She has a narrower smokestack and is fitted with an SQS-23 sonar—the only US carrier so equipped. ▶

Below: *Constellation* **(CV-64) during underway replenishment operations with an oiler of the Mispillion class and a missile destroyer of the Charles F. Adams class.**

▶ In 1963 it was decided that the new carrier due to be laid down in FY 1964 would be nuclear-powered, but Congress baulked at the cost, and the ship was finally laid down as a conventionally powered carrier of a modified Kitty Hawk design. *John F. Kennedy* can be distinguished externally from her near-sisters by her canted stack—designed to keep the corrosive exhaust gases clear of the flight deck—and by the shape of the forward end of the angled deck.

Of even greater significance was the abandonment of the expensive long-range Terrier system, which took up valuable space and merely duplicated similar area defence systems on the carrier escorts, in favour of the Basic Point Defence Missile System (BPDMS), for which three octuple launchers were fitted. The SPS-48 radar, carried on a rather slimmer mast aft of the island, was fitted from the outset. Provision was made, as in *America*, for an SQS-23 sonar, but this was never installed.

John F. Kennedy marks the high point of US carrier construction, and it is significant that the later CVNs of the Nimitz class are almost identical in flight-deck layout, armament, and sensor outfit. The earlier three ships of the Kitty Hawk class are now being refitted to the same standard. In particular the Terrier launchers, together with the fire control radars, are being removed and replaced by Mk 29 launchers for NATO Sea Sparrow. It is envisaged that all four ships will eventually carry three Mk 29 launchers and three Phalanx CIWS guns. All vessels in the class are now fitted with the SPS-48 3-D radar, and the SPS-37A air search radar is being replaced by the much more compact SPS-49.

Kitty Hawk and *Constellation* have served since completion in the Pacific. *America* and *John F. Kennedy* serve in the Atlantic, with frequent deployments to the Mediterranean.

Above: An aerial view of *America* (CV-66) testing the washdown system which would protect her from nuclear fall-out.

Below: *John F. Kennedy* (CVN-67). Note the distinctive canted smoke-stack. Aircraft include F-14, A-7 and A-6.

CV
Forrestal

Completed: 1952-5.
Names: CV 59 *Forrestal;* CV 60 *Saratoga;* CV 61 *Ranger;*
CV 62 *Independence.*
Displacement: 60,000t standard; 78,000t full load.
Dimensions: 1,039-1,047 oa x 130wl, 238 flight deck x 37ft
(316.7-319 x 38.5, 72.5 x 11.3m).
Propulsion: 4-shaft geared steam turbines; 260-280,000shp = 33kts.
Armament: CV 59-60: 2 BPDMS launchers Mk 25 (2x8);
CV 61-62: 2 NATO Sea Sparrow launchers Mk 29 (2x8).
Aircraft: 24 F-4J Phantom; 24 A-7E Corsair; 10 A-6E Intruder
+ 4 KA-6D; 4 E-2C Hawkeye; 4 EA-6B Prowler;
10 S-3A Viking; 6 SH-3H Sea King.
Sensors: *Surveillance:* SPS-48, SPS-43A, SPS-10, SPS-58
(not in CV 61).
Fire Control: 2 Mk 115 (CV 59-60), 2 Mk 91 (CV 61-62).

Authorisation of the Forrestal class was a direct consequence of the Korean
War, which re-established the value of the carrier for projecting air power
against land targets. The new class was to operate the A-3 Skywarrior
strategic bomber, which weighed fully 78,000lb (35,455kg) and dimensions
and hangar height were increased accordingly. The original design was for a
carrier similar in configuration to the ill-fated *United States,* which had a
flush deck, together with a retractable bridge, and two waist catapults
angled out on sponsons in addition to the standard pair of catapults forward. ▶

Above: *Saratoga* (CV-60) underway. She is at present undergoing a major refit as part of the Service Life Extension Programme.

Below: *Forrestal* (CV-59) underway in the Mediterranean. Unlike more recent carriers she continues to operate the F-4 Phantom.

► The advent of the angled deck, which was tested by the US Navy in 1952 on the Essex-class carrier *Antietam*, led to the modification of *Forrestal* while building to incorporate this new development. The result was the distinctive configuration which has been adopted by all subsequent US carrier construction: a massive flight deck with considerable overhang supported by sponsons to the sides, with a small island incorporating the smokestack to starboard. The Forrestals were the first US carriers to have the flight deck as the strength deck – in previous ships it was the hangar deck – and in consequence side lifts were adopted in preference to centreline lifts and

incorporated in the overhang. This resulted in a large uninterrupted hangar in which more than half the ship's aircraft could be struck down. The layout of the four side lifts proved less than satisfactory, however; in particular the port-side lift, which is at the forward end of the angled deck, cannot be used during landing operations, and the Kitty Hawk class which followed had a modified arrangement.

All four ships of the class were completed with eight 5-inch (127mm) single mountings on sponsons fore and aft. The forward sponsons created problems in heavy seas, however, and the three ships based in the Atlantic had both guns and sponsons removed in the early 1960s (*Ranger* lost her forward guns but retained the sponsons). During the 1970s all guns were replaced by BPDMS Mk 25 or IPDMS Mk 29 launchers. Eventually all four ships will have three Mk 29 launchers and three Phalanx CIWS guns.

The electronics suite has undergone considerable change and expansion since the 1950s. Large SPS-43A long-range air search aerials have been fitted on outriggers to the starboard side of the island, and the distinctive SPS-30 3-D radar was carried above the bridge from the early 1960s until replaced in the late 1970s by the SPS-48. *Saratoga* was taken in hand in October 1980 for a 3-year major modernisation (SLEP) which will include replacement of the SPS-43 by the new SPS-49.

Unlike later carriers, the Forrestal class do not operate the F-14 Tomcat, but retain the F-4 Phantom. It is envisaged that the latter will eventually be replaced by the F-18 Hornet.

Left: *Independence* (CV-62) operating in the Mediterranean. A BPDMS launcher can be seen below the level of the flight deck.

Below: A recent view of *Forrestal* (CV-59). She now has the SPS-48 planar radar above the bridge in place of the SPS-30.

CV

Midway

Completed:	1945-7.
Names:	CV 41 *Midway;* CV 43 *Coral Sea.*
Displacement:	51-52,000t standard; 64,000t full load.
Dimensions:	979 oa x 121 wl, 259/236 flight deck x 36ft (298.4 x 36.9, 78.8/71.9 x 11m).
Propulsion:	4-shaft geared steam turbines; 212,000shp = 32kts.
Armament:	2 BPDMS launchers Mk 25 (2x8–CV 41 only); 3 Phalanx CIWS.
Aircraft:	24 F-4J Phantom; 24 A-7E Corsair; 10 A-6E Intruder + 4 KA-6D; 4 E-2C Hawkeye; 4 EA-6B Prowler.
Sensors:	*Surveillance:* (CV 41) SPS-48A, SPS-37A, SPS-10; (CV 43) SPS-30, SPS-43A, SPS-10. *Fire Control:* 2 Mk 115.

These ships were the last war-built US carriers. Three units were completed but *Franklin D. Roosevelt* was stricken in 1977. As built, the Midway class had an axial flight deck with two centre-line lifts and a side lift amidships on the port side. They were armed with a heavy battery of 14-18 5-inch (127mm) guns and numerous smaller AA weapons. The original design was quickly overtaken by developments in jet aircraft, and the class underwent a major modernisation during the 1950s in which an 8-degree angled deck was built, incorporating the side lift at its forward end; the after lift, which would have obstructed landing operations, was removed and replaced by a second side lift to starboard aft of the island. The armament was significantly reduced and the latest 3-D and air search radars fitted. C-11 steam catapults were installed to enable the ships to operate the new generation of various types of jet aircraft. ▶

Right: *Midway* **(CV-41) operating in the Western Pacific. She is the only US carrier home-ported outside the United States.**

Below: Aerial view of *Coral Sea* **(CV-43). Aircraft on deck include F-4s, A-7s, A-6s and the E-2C Hawkeye AEW aircraft.**

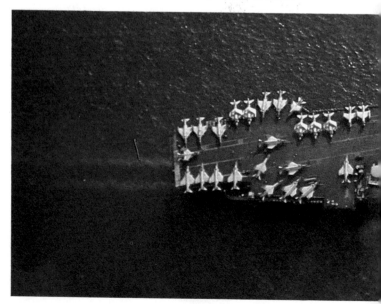

► *Coral Sea*, which was the last of the three to the modernised, incorporated a number of further modifications as a result of experience with her two sisters and with the Forrestal class. The position of the port-side lift was found to be unsatisfactory, and it was moved aft to clear the angled deck altogether. This enabled the angled deck itself to be extended forward with a consequent increase in deck space, and a third C-11 catapult was installed. The position of the forward centre-line lift was found to be equally unsatisfactory, as it was situated between the forward catapults and was therefore unusable during take-off operations. It was therefore removed and replaced by a third side lift forward of the island. New sponsons were built for the six remaining guns, which were now just below flight-deck level.

The conversion of *Coral Sea* was particularly successful, and she remained largely unaltered–except for the removal of the remaining guns–throughout the following two decades. Since 1978 she has been the thirteenth carrier in a 12-carrier force and has only recently been reactivated to replace *Saratoga* while the latter undergoes her SLEP.

In 1966 *Midway* was taken in hand for a major modernisation which would enable her to operate the same aircraft as the more modern US carriers. The flight deck was completely rebuilt–its total area was increased by approximately one-third–and the lifts rearranged on the pattern established by *Coral Sea* (The new lifts are much larger, however, and have a capacity of 130,000lb (59,100kg) compared with 74,000lb (33,636kg) for those of her sister-ship). Two C-13 catapults were installed forward, enabling *Midway* to handle the latest aircraft. The armament was reduced to three 5-inch (127mm) guns (these were replaced in 1979 by two BPDMS launchers). NTDS was installed during the modernisation and the island has recently been extended to incorporate the latest sensors. Three Phalanx CIWS guns are to be fitted in the near future.

Midway, which is based in Japan, is due to remain in service until 1988, when she will replace *Coral Sea* as a training ship. Her principal limitations compared with later carriers are those inherent in the initial design; a hangar height of only 5.3m (17ft 6in)–the E-2 Hawkeye AEW aircraft needs 5.6m (18ft 4in) clearance–and a limited aviation fuel capacity–365,000 gallons compared with 750,000 gallons in the Forrestal design. In spite of their CV designation neither *Midway* nor *Coral Sea* operate fixed- or rotary-wing ASW aircraft, and both continue to operate the F-4 Phantom in place of the F-14 Tomcat.

Below: A Soviet AGI shadows *Coral Sea* (CV-43) in the Gulf of Tonkin during the Vietnam War. An A-3 Skywarrior is refuelling.

Bottom: *Midway* (CV-41) now has a new lattice mast aft of the funnel. It is intended to fit the planar SPS-48 3-D radar.

Cruisers

Ticonderoga

Completed: 1983 onwards.
Names: CG 47 *Ticonderoga;* CG 48 *Yorktown;* CG 49. . . .;
CG 50. . . .; CG 51. . . .; CG 52. . . .
Displacement: 9,100t full load.
Dimensions: 563 oa x 55 x 31ft (171.7 x 17 x 17.6 x 9.4m).
Propulsion: 2-shaft COGAG; 4 LM2500 gas turbines;
80,000bhp = 30kts.
Armament: *AAW:* 2 twin Mk 26 launchers (44 + 44) for Standard MR
SM-2 missiles; 2 5-inch (127mm) Mk 45 (2x1);
2 Phalanx CIWS.
ASW: ASROC missiles from Mk 26 launcher;
2 LAMPS helicopters; 6 12.75-inch (324mm) torpedo
tubes Mk 32 (2x3).
SSM: 8 Harpoon missiles (2x4).
Sensors: *Surveillance:* 4 SPY-1A, SPS-49, SPS-55.
Fire Control: 4 Mk 99, SPQ-9A.
Sonars: SQS-53A, SQR-19 TACTAS.

Most of the cruisers in the US Fleet were completed during the 1960s. Their missiles and electronics have received constant updates to enable them to keep abreast of the threat to the carrier battle groups posed by long-range Soviet bombers. Conventional air defence systems are now considered inadequate to meet this threat and a large programme of new cruisers armed with the revolutionary AEGIS system is now uderway. Five are on order and 18 more figure in the 1982-87 programme.

The new missile cruiser *Ticonderoga* will be the first operational vessel to be fitted with the AEGIS Combat System. It was originally envisaged that this system would be installed in nuclear-powered escorts such as the Strike Cruiser (CSGN) and the CGN 42 variant of the Virginia class, but the enormous cost of AEGIS combined with that of nuclear propulsion proved to be prohibitive under the restrictive budgets of the late 1970s. Moreover, two AEGIS escorts were required for each of the twelve carrier battle groups, and as not all of the carriers concerned were nuclear-powered, it was decided to utilise the growth potential of the fossil-fuelled Spruance design to incorporate the necessary electronics.

The AEGIS Combat System was developed to counter the saturation missile attacks which could be expected to form the basis of Soviet anti-carrier tactics during the 1980s. Conventional rotating radars are limited both in data rate and in number of target tracks they can handle, whereas saturation missile attacks require sensors which can react immediately and have a virtually unlimited tracking capacity. The solution adopted in the AEGIS system is to mount four fixed planar antennae each covering a sector of 45 degrees on the superstructures of the ship. Each SPY-1 array has ▶

Below: *Ticonderoga* (CG-47), the first of the new AEGIS cruisers, is docked after her launch at the Ingalls Yard.

▶ more than 4000 radiating elements that shape and direct multiple beams. Targets satisfying predetermined criteria are evaluated, arranged in sequence of threat and engaged, either automatically or with manual override, by a variety of defensive systems.

At longer ranges air targets will be engaged by the SM-2 missile, fired from one of two Mk 26 launchers. The SM-2 differs from previous missiles in requiring target illumination only in the terminal phase of flight. In the initial and mid-flight phase the missile flies under auto-pilot towards a predicted interception point with initial guidance data and limited mid-course guidance supplied by the AEGIS system. This means that no less than 18 missiles can be kept in the air in addition to the four in the terminal phase, and the Mk 99 illuminators switch rapidly from one target to the next under computer control. At closer ranges back-up is provided by the two 5-inch guns, while "last-ditch" self-defence is provided by two Phalanx CIWS guns, assisted by ECM jammers and chaff dispensers.

Ticonderoga and her sisters are designed to serve as flagships, and will be equipped with an elaborate Combat Information Centre (CIC) possessing an integral flag function able to accept and coordinate data from other ships and aircraft. Eighteen units are currently projected, and it is envisaged that they will operate in conjunction with specialised ASW destroyers of the Spruance class and a new type of AAW destroyer (the DDGX).

Above right: Port bow view of *Ticonderoga* (CG-47) prior to launching. The basic design is that of the Spruance-class DD.

Below: Starboard quarter view of *Ticonderoga* (CG-47) prior to launch. One of the large CP propellers is visible.

Ticonderoga (CG-47).

Virginia

Completed:	1976-80.
Names:	CGN 38 *Virginia;* CGN 39 *Texas;* CGN 40 *Mississippi;* CGN 41 *Arkansas.*
Displacement:	11,000t full load.
Dimensions:	585 oa x 63 x 30ft (178 x 19 x 9m).
Propulsion:	2-shaft nuclear; 2 D2G reactors; 60,000shp = 30kts.
Armament:	*AAW:* 2 twin Mk 26 launchers (44 + 24) for Standard MR missiles; 2 5-inch (127mm) Mk 45 (2x1).
	ASW: 1 LAMPS helicopter (see notes); ASROC missiles from fwd Mk 26 launcher; 6 12.75-inch (324mm) torpedo tubes Mk 32 (2x3).
	SSM: 8 Harpoon missiles (2x4) being fitted.
Sensors:	*Surveillance:* SPS-48C, SPS-40B, SPS-55.
	Fire Control: 2 SPG-51D, SPG-60, SPQ-9A.
	Sonars: SQS-53A.

Following closely upon the two CGNs of the California class, the *Virginia* incorporated a number of significant modifications. While the basic layout of the class is identical to that of their predecessors, the single-arm Mk 13 launchers of the *California* were superseded by the new Mk 26 twin

ASROC launcher forward, and a helicopter hangar was built into the stern.

The magazine layout and missile-handling arrangements of the Mk 26 constitute a break with previous US Navy practice. In earlier missile cruisers and destroyers booster-assisted missiles such as Terrier were stowed in horizontal magazine rings, and the shorter Tartar missiles in cylindrical magazines comprising two concentric rings of vertically stowed missiles. The magazine associated with the Mk 26 launcher, however, has a continuous belt feed system with vertical stowage capable of accommodating a variety of missiles. This means that ship's length is the only limiting factor on the size of the magazine, which is capable of being "stretched" or "contracted" to suit the dimensions of the vessel in which it is to be installed. It has also eliminated the requirement for a separate launcher for ASROC. In the Virginia class ASROC rounds are carried in the forward magazine alongside Standard MR surface-to-air missiles. The elimination of the ASROC launcher and its associated reloading deckhouse has saved 5m (16.4ft) in length compared with *California*.

The installation of an internal helicopter hangar in a ship other than an aircraft carrier is unique in the postwar US Navy. The hangar itself is 42ft by 14ft (12.8 x 4.3m) and is served by a stern elevator covered by a folding hatch. Although it is envisaged that SH-2F helicopters will eventually be ▶

Below: *Virginia* (CGN-38) underway. The class was designed to escort the nuclear-powered carriers of the Nimitz class.

Above: Stern view of *Mississippi* (CGN-40). The twin-arm Mk 26 launchers distinguish her from the earlier California class.

▶ assigned, the ships do not at present have helicopters embarked.

The electronics outfit is on a par with *California*, with two important differences. The first is the replacement of the SQS-26 sonar by the more advanced solid-state SQS-53, and the older Mk 114 ASW FC system by the digital Mk 116. The second is the retention of only the after pair of SPG 51 tracker/illuminators, reducing the number of available channels (including the SPG-60) from five to three. This modification looks forward to the conversion of the ships to fire the SM-2 missile, which requires target illumination only in the terminal phase. The ships are also scheduled to receive Harpoon, Tomahawk, and two Phalanx CIWS guns at future refits.

The original requirement was for eleven ships of this class, which would then combine with earlier CGNs to provide each of the CVANs projected at that time with four nuclear-powered escorts. After only four units of the class had been laid down, however, further orders were suspended while consideration was given first to the Strike Cruiser (CSGN) and then to a modified CGN 38 design with AEGIS. Both these projects were abandoned in favour of the conventionally powered CG-47 now under construction, but the CGN42 AEGIS proposal has recently been revived.

All four ships of the Virginia class currently serve with the Atlantic Fleet, where they have the job of protecting the carriers *Nimitz* and *Eisenhower*.

Texas (CGN-39).

Below: *Virginia* (CGN-38) underway in the Indian Ocean. Nuclear power makes these ships well-suited to long-range operations.

California

Completed:	1974-5.
Names:	CGN 36 *California;* CGN 37 *South Carolina.*
Displacement:	10,150t full load.
Dimensions:	596 oa x 61 x 32ft (182 x 18.6 x 9.6m).
Propulsion:	2-shaft nuclear, 2 D2G reactors; 60,000shp = 30kts.
Armament:	*AAW:* 2 single Mk 13 launchers (40 + 40) Standard MR missiles, 2 5-inch (127mm) Mk 45 (2x1).
	ASW: ASROC launcher Mk 16 (1x8, reloads); 4 12.75-inch (324mm) torpedo tubes (4x1, fixed).
	SSM: 8 Harpoon missiles (2x4) being fitted.
Sensors:	*Surveillance:* SPS-48C, SPS-40B, SPS-10.
	Fire Control: 4 SPG-51D, SPG-60, SPQ-9A.
	Sonars: SQS-26CX.

California and her sister *South Carolina* were built in response to the need for a new class of nuclear escorts to accompany the CVNs of the *Nimitz* class. A third ship was approved in FY 1968, but this was later cancelled in favour of the improved *Virginia* design.

Compared with previous CGNs, *California* is a much larger, more sophisticated vessel. The design reverted to the "double-ended" layout of *Bainbridge,* but single Mk 13 Tartar launchers were adopted in preference to the Mk 10. This was in some ways a retrograde step in that it limited the ships to the medium-range (MR) version of the Standard missile, whereas earlier

CGs and CGNs could be retro-fitted with the extended-range (ER) version. It also necessitated the provision of a separate ASROC launcher, forward of which there is a magazine surmounted by a prominent deckhouse into which the missiles are hoisted before reloading.

California was the first ship to be fitted with the new lightweight 5-inch (127mm) gun, and the first to have the digital Mk 86 FC system installed. The anti-surface element of the latter—the SPQ-9 antenna—is housed within a radome on the after side of the mainmast, while the SPG-60 antenna, which besides tracking air targets can serve as a fifth illuminating channel for the missiles, is located directly above the bridge.

Both ships have served in the Atlantic since completion. They will be fitted with Harpoon, Tomahawk, and two Phalanx CIWS guns at future refits.

California (CGN-36).

Below: *California* **(CGN-36) underway off Puerto Rico. Note the single Mk 13 launchers which distinguish her from later CGNs.** *California* **was the first US ship to receive the 5-inch Mk 45 together with the digital Mk 86 fire control system.**

Truxtun

Completed: 1967.
Name: CGN 35 *Truxtun*.
Displacement: 8,200t standard; 9,200t full load.
Dimensions: 564 oa x 58 x 31ft (172 x 17.7 x 9.4m).
Propulsion: 2-shaft nuclear; 2 D2G reactors; 60,000shp = 30kts.
Armament: *AAW:* twin Mk 10 launcher (60) for Standard ER missiles;
1 5-inch (127mm) Mk 42.
ASW: ASROC missiles from Mk 10 launcher;
1 SH-2F helicopter; 4 12.75-inch (324mm) torpedo tubes
Mk 32 (4x1, fixed).
SSM: 8 Harpoon missiles (2x4).
Sensors: *Surveillance:* SPS-48, SPS-40, SPS-10.
Fire Control: 2 SPG-55B, 1 SPG-53F.
Sonars: SQS-26.

Originally requested as one of seven Belknap-class frigates in the FY 1962 programme, *Truxtun* was given nuclear propulsion at the insistence of Congress. She emerged from the drawing board with tall, distinctive lattice masts in place of the twin macks of the oil-burning ships.

While she carried an identical weapons outfit to her near-sisters, major modifications were made to the layout. The positions of the Mk 10 launcher and the 5-inch (127mm) Mk 42 and their respective fire-control radars were reversed, and the ASROC/Terrier magazine rings were therefore located beneath the flight deck and not forward of the bridge. In place of the triple Mk 32 torpedo tubes of the Belknaps *Truxtun* has two fixed tubes located in the superstructure on either side amidships. The helicopter hangar, which is

40ft by 17ft (12.3 x 5m), is shorter and wider than that of the Belknaps.

Truxtun originally had twin 3-inch (76mm) mountings amidships, but these were replaced in the late 1970s by quadruple launchers for Harpoon. The two Mk 25 stern tubes have also been removed. Two Phalanx CIWS guns will be fitted in the near future.

Truxtun has served since completion in the Pacific Fleet, where she has combined with *Long Beach* and *Bainbridge* to form the nuclear-powered escort squadron which accompanies the carrier *Enterprise.*

Below: *Truxtun* (CGN-35) underway in the Pacific. Note the distinctive lattice masts which carry the surveillance radars.

Bottom: Port-side view of *Truxtun*. Her armament is similar to that of the Belknap class but the layout is reversed.

Belknap

Completed: 1964-7.
Names: CG 26 *Belknap;* CG 27 *Josephus Daniels;*
CG 28 *Wainwright;* CG 29 *Jouett;* CG 30 *Horne;*
CG 31 *Sterett;* CG 32 *William H. Standley;* CG 33 *Fox;*
CG 34 *Biddle.*
Displacement: 6,570t standard; 7,930t full load.
Dimensions: 547 oa x 55 x 29ft (166.7 x 16.7 x 8.7m).
Propulsion: 2-shaft geared steam turbines; 85,000shp = 33kts.
Armament: *AAW:* twin Mk 10 launcher (60) for Standard ER missiles;
1 5-inch (127mm) Mk 42; 2 Phalanx CIWS being fitted.
ASW: ASROC missiles from Mk 10 launcher;
1 SH-2F helicopter; 6 12.75-inch (324mm) torpedo
tubes Mk 32 (2x3).
SSM: 8 Harpoon missiles (2x4).
Sensors: *Surveillance:* SPS-48, SPS-40 (CG 29, 31-34) *or*
SPS-43 (CG 27-28, 30) *or* SPS-49 (CG 26), SPS-10F.
Fire Control: 2 SPG-55B, 1 SPG-53.
Sonars: SQS-26BX (except CG 26, SQS-53C)

The nine ships of the Belknap class, together with their nuclear-powered half-sister *Truxtun*, constitute the final group of AAW "frigates" completed for the US Navy during the 1960s. Outwardly they resemble their predecessors of the Leahy class, with which they share a common hull-form and superstructure layout. A closer look, however, reveals a shift in emphasis in favour of significantly increased anti-submarine capabilities.

In the Belknaps the "double-ended" missile launcher arrangement was abandoned and the 5-inch gun reinstated—a reflection, in part, of concern about the diminishing number of vessels capable of fire support operations. The Mk 10 Terrier launcher was given a third 20-round magazine ring located below and between the other two. The extra capacity was used, however, not to compensate for the reduction in Terrier rounds compared with the *Leahy,* but in order to dispense with a separate ASROC launcher. The upper two rings carry alternate Terrier/Standard and ASROC rounds, while the third, which carries only SAM rounds, serves as a feed for the two upper rings.

The additional deck space gained as a result of these modifications was utilised to provide a helicopter platform and hangar immediately aft of the ▶

Below: *William H. Standley* (CG-32) in the Mediterranean. The Mk 10 launcher fires both Standard ER and ASROC missiles.

▶ second mack. It was envisaged that the Belknaps would operate the ill-fated drone anti-submarine helicopter (DASH) but the programme was abandoned before any drones were embarked. Instead, the Belknaps became the trial class for the LAMPS helicopter programme in the early 1970s, and introduced manned ASW helicopters to the US Navy with conspicuous success.

Wainwright (CG-28).

Below: Aerial view of *Jouett* (CG-29) off Hawaii. The Belknap class is the standard conventional AAW escort in the US Navy.

Below right: Stern view of a Belknap. Note the 5-inch gun.

The Belknaps carried an altogether more advanced electronics outfit to the Leahy class. In particular the SQS-23 sonar was replaced by the much more powerful SQS-26, while the new planar SPS-48 3-D radar replaced the older SPS-39. Target and fire control data were coordinated by the US Navy's first computer-based Naval Tactical Data System (NTDS). Moreover, these systems have been constantly updated in order to keep abreast of the aerial threat. Since 1977 *Wainwright* has been modified to conduct evaluation of the SM-2 missile, which will eventually be carried by all ships of the class. *Belknap,* which had her entire upper works destroyed by fire following a collision with the carrier *John F. Kennedy* in 1975, has been rebuilt with a completely updated sensor outfit, including an SPS-49 air search radar, an SQS-53A sonar, and SLQ-32(V)3 ECM antennae. All ships have now been fitted with quadruple Harpoon launchers in place of the former 3-inch (76mm) AA guns amidships, and each will receive two Phalanx CIWS guns in the near future.

Four units of the Belknap class currently serve in the Atlantic, and five in the Pacific. They are employed as AAW escorts for the conventionally powered carriers.

Bainbridge

Completed: 1962.
Names: CGN 25 *Bainbridge*.
Displacement: 7,700t standard; 8,580t full load.
Dimensions: 565 oa x 58 x 29ft (172.5 x 17.7 x 7.9m).
Propulsion: 2-shaft nuclear; 2 D2G reactors; 60,000shp = 30kts.
Armament: *AAW:* 2 twin Mk 10 launchers (40 + 40) for Standard
ER missiles; 2 20mm (2x1).
ASW: ASROC launcher Mk 16 (1x8);
6 12.75-inch (324mm) torpedo tubes Mk 32 (2x3).
SSM: 8 Harpoon missiles (2x4).
Sensors: *Surveillance:* SPS-48, SPS-37, SPS-10D.
Fire Control: 4 SPG-55B.
Sonars: SQS-23.

Like the later *Truxtun, Bainbridge* is an offshoot of a larger class of conventionally powered AAW "frigates". She is a near-sister of the Leahy class, with which she initially shared an identical outfit of weapons and electronics. As completed, she presented a more streamlined profile than the *Leahy* because her nuclear propulsion enabled her to dispense with the tall macks of the latter.

The layout of *Bainbridge's* weapons is identical to that of the *Leahy,* with twin Mk 10 Terrier launchers fore and aft and an ASROC box launcher forward of the bridge. From 1974 onwards the ship underwent an extensive refit aimed at upgrading her electronics. The refit included not only the installation of new surveillance radars and NTDS but also the complete remodelling of her superstructure, which now comprises two distinct blocks with much greater internal volume. The forward block is surmounted by a broad lattice mast and the after block by a heavy pole mainmast. The former 3-inch (76mm) AA guns have been replaced by quadruple Harpoon launchers, and two Phalanx CIWS guns will be fitted abreast the after SPG-55 tracker/illuminators in the near future.

Bainbridge has served since completion in the Pacific, where she has combined with *Truxtun* and *Long Beach* to form the nuclear-powered escort squadron which accompanies the carrier *Enterprise*.

Above: *Bainbridge* (CGN-25) was the US Navy's first nuclear-powered AAW escort. She has recently undergone modernisation.

Below: *Bainbridge* underway in the Pacific. Note the "double-ended" missile launcher layout and the absence of major guns.

Leahy

Completed: 1962-4.
Names: CG 16 *Leahy;* CG 17 *Harry E. Yarnell;* CG 18 *Worden;* CG 19 *Dale;* CG 20 *Richmond K. Turner;* CG 21 *Gridley;* CG 22 *England;* CG 23 *Halsey;* CG 24 *Reeves.*
Displacement: 5,670t standard; 7,800t full load.
Dimensions: 553 oa x 55 x 25ft (162.5 x 16.8 x 7.6m).
Propulsion: 2-shaft geared steam turbines; 85,000shp = 32kts.
Armament: *AAW:* 2 twin Mk 10 launchers (40 + 40) for Standard ER missiles; 4 3-inch (76mm, 2x2) in some ships; 2 Phalanx CIWS being fitted.
ASW: ASROC launcher Mk 16 (1x8); 6 12.75-inch (324mm) torpedo tubes Mk 32 (2x3).
SSM: 8 Harpoon missiles (2x4) being fitted in place 3-inch (76mm) guns.
Sensors: *Surveillance:* SPS-48, SPS-43 (SPS-49 in CG 19), SPS-10. *Fire Control:* 4 SPG-55B. *Sonars:* SQS-23.

The nine ships of the Leahy class, together with their nuclear-powered half-sister *Bainbridge,* constitute the second group of AAW "frigates" completed for the US Navy during the 1960s. They were designed at a time when it was thought that guns would disappear altogether from the inventory of naval weapons. They were therefore the first US Navy ships to have an all-missile main armament. They also introduced the "mack" (combined mast and stack) to US Navy construction as a means of conserving valuable centre-line deck space. ▶

Right: Stern view of *Leahy* (CG-16) in the Pacific. The class underwent a major AAW modernisation in the early 1970s.

Below: The cruiser *Halsey* (CG-23). The "double-ended" missile launcher layout distinguishes her from the later Belknap class.

▶ A "double-ended" layout was adopted with twin Mk 10 Terrier launchers fore and aft. There are 20-round magazine rings in line with each launcher arm, and the missiles are lifted from the top of the ring and run up at an angle of 15 degrees through a wedge-shaped deckhouse onto the launcher. Target tracking and illumination are provided by paired SPG-55B FC radars mounted atop the fore and after superstructures.

As in the earlier Coontz class, there is an 8-round ASROC launcher forward of the bridge, but no reloads are carried.

From 1967 until 1972 the Leahy class underwent an extensive modernisation programme aimed at bringing their electronics up to the same standard as the Belknaps. A large planar SPS-48 3-D radar replaced the original SPS-39, and NTDS was installed. *Dale* has now received the new SPS-49 air search radar in place of her SPS-43, and this modification will eventually be extended to all ships of this class and the Belknap class.

Several ships have already had their 3-inch (76mm) AA guns removed, and they are scheduled to receive Harpoon in their place. They will also receive two Phalanx CIWS guns.

Only three units of this class are based in the Atlantic, the remaining six being allocated to the Pacific Fleet. These dispositions are almost certainly related to their much greater cruising range as compared with the preceding Coontz class, and also to their limited ASW capabilities. Two of these AAW ships would normally be allocated to each non-nuclear carrier battle group.

Dale **(CG-19).**

Above: *Leahy* (CG-16) underway in the Pacific. The large planar antenna atop the foremast is an SPS-48 3-D radar.

Below: *Halsey* (CG-23) in the Pacific. Only three ships of the class serve with the Atlantic Fleet.

Long Beach

Completed: 1961.
Name: CGN 9 *Long Beach.*
Displacement: 14,200t standard; 17,350t full load.
Dimensions: 721 oa x 73 x 29ft (219.8 x 22.3 x 8.8m).
Propulsion: 2-shaft nuclear; 2 C1W reactors; 80,000shp = 30kts.
Armament: *AAW:* 2 twin Mk 10 launchers (40 + 80) for Standard ER missiles; 2 5-inch (127mm) Mk 30 (2x1).
ASW: ASROC launcher Mk 16 (1x8); 6 12.75-inch (324mm) torpedo tubes Mk 32 (2x3).
SSM: 8 Harpoon missiles (2x4).
Sensors: *Surveillance:* SPS-48C, SPS-49, SPS-65.
Fire Control: 4 SPG-55A.
Sonars: SQQ-23.

Long Beach was the US Navy's first all-missile warship, and the first surface ship with nuclear power. She was designed as an escort for the carrier *Enterprise,* and has performed this role throughout the past two decades

As completed she had two Mk 10 Terrier launchers forward and a Mk 12 launcher aft for the long-range Talos. The depth of the hull enabled an extra pair of magazine rings to be worked in beneath the second Mk 10 launcher, giving *Long Beach* a total capacity of no less than 166 surface-to-air missiles. There was an ASROC box launcher amidships, and shortly after the ship entered service two 5-inch (127mm) guns of an older pattern were fitted to provide defence against small surface craft.

Electronics were on a par with *Enterprise* herself, with large fixed SPS-32/33 "billboard" radars mounted on a similar "turret" superstructure block. The latter proved to be a major maintenance problem, and the FY 1978 budget provided funds to fit *Long Beach* with the AEGIS system. The proposed conversion was quickly cancelled, however, as it was feared that this expenditure might result in reductions in the new CG 47 programme.

Talos was removed in 1979 and the after launcher replaced by quadruple Harpoon launchers. The following year *Long Beach* began a major refit at which the SPS-32/33 radars will be removed and their functions taken over by an SPS-48 3-D radar and an SPS-49 air search radar—the latter atop lattice mainmast. Two Phalanx CIWS guns will be installed on the after superstructure, and there will eventually be launchers for Tomahawk aft.

Below: Aerial view of *Long Beach* (CGN-9) underway in the Pacific. The Talos launcher has already been removed.

Bottom: *Long Beach* comes alongside at San Diego. in her current refit the SPS-32 and SPS-33 planar radars are being removed.

Destroyers

Kidd

Completed:	1981-2.
Names:	DDG 993 *Kidd;* DDG 994 *Callaghan;* DDG 995 *Scott;* DDG 996 *Chandler.*
Displacement:	8,140t full load.
Dimensions:	563 oa x 55 x 30ft (171.1 x 16.8 x 8.1m).
Propulsion:	2-shaft COGAG; 4 LM2500 gas turbines; 80,000bhp = 30kts.
Armament:	*AAW:* 2 twin Mk 26 launchers (24 + 44) for Standard MR missiles; 2 5-inch (127mm) Mk 45 (2x1).
	ASW: ASROC missiles from Mk 26 launcher; 2 LAMPS helicopters; 6 12.75-inch (324mm) torpedo tubes Mk 32 (2x3).
	SSM: 8 Harpoon missiles (2x4).
Sensors:	*Surveillance:* SPS-48, SPS-55.
	Fire Control: 2 SPG-51, SPG-60, SPQ-9A.
	Sonars: SQS-53.

The four ships of the Kidd class are AAW modifications of the Spruance-class destroyer originally ordered by Iran but acquired by the US Navy in 1979 following the fall of the Shah.

The allowances made in the Spruance design for the modular installation of a number of weapon systems then in production or under development made redesign a simple matter, as the AAW modification had been one of the variations originally envisaged. In the Kidd class twin-arm Mk 26 launchers have been fitted fore and aft in place of the ASROC and Sea Sparrow launchers of the ASW version. The forward magazine is the smaller of the two, the original intention being to fit the now-defunct 8-inch (205mm) Mk 71 gun in place of the forward 5-inch (127mm) mounting. Contrary to US Navy practice, an SPS-48 3-D radar is fitted, but there is no independent air

Callaghan (DDG-994).

In the US Fleet structure the destroyer is a fleet unit, with adequate speed to keep pace with a carrier battle group. Destroyers are divided into those with an air defence function (DDG) and those with an antisubmarine mission (DD). Most of the DDGs were completed in the early 1960's and therefore need replacing in the not-so-distant future. The ASW destroyers of the Spruance class, however, are large modern units. The older DDGs—and CGs— will eventually be replaced by a new design, the DDGX.

search radar. There are also only two SPG-51 tracker/illuminators—one above the bridge and the other on a raised superstructure immediately abaft the mainmast. The electronics outfit is therefore austere by US Navy standards, but this will be remedied over the next few years by the addition of systems currently being fitted to other ships of similar capabilities. Two Phalanx CIWS guns are to be fitted in the near future.

The Kidd-class destroyers can fire ASROC missiles from their forward Mk 26 launcher, resulting in an ASW capability not far short of that of the standard Spruance.

The provision of extra air-conditioning capacity and dust separators for the gas-turbine air intakes makes these ships well suited to operations in tropical conditions.

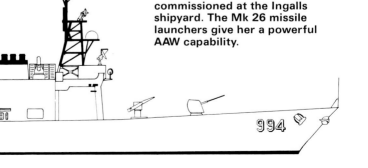

Above: *Kidd* **(DDG-993), the first ship of the class, is commissioned at the Ingalls shipyard. The Mk 26 missile launchers give her a powerful AAW capability.**

Spruance

Completed: 1975-80.
Names: DD 963 *Spruance;* DD 964 *Paul F. Foster;* DD 965 *Kinkaid;*
DD 966 *Hewitt;* DD 967 *Elliott;*
DD 968 *Arthur W. Radford;* DD 969 *Peterson;*
DD 970 *Caron;* DD 971 *David W. Ray;* DD 972 *Oldendorf;*
DD 973 *John Young;* DD 974 *Comte De Grasse;*
DD 975 *O'Brien;* DD 976 *Merrill;* DD 977 *Briscoe;*
DD 978 *Stump;* DD 979 *Conolly;* DD 980 *Moosbrugger;*
DD 981 *John Hancock;* DD 982 *Nicholson;*
DD 983 *John Rodgers;* DD 984 *Leftwich;* DD 985 *Cushing;*
DD 986 *Harry W. Hill;* DD 987 *O'Bannon;* DD 988 *Thorn;*
DD 989 *Deyo;* DD 990 *Ingersoll;* DD 991 *Fife;*
DD 992 *Fletcher;* DD 997 *Hayler* (building).
Displacement: 7,800t full load.
Dimensions: 563 oa x 55 x 29ft (171.1 x 16.8 x 8.8m).
Propulsion: 2-shaft COGAG; 4 LM2500 gas turbines;
80,000bhp = 30 + kts.

Armament: ASW: ASROC launcher Mk 16 (1x8, 24 reloads);
                  2 SH-2F helicopters (only one embarked); 6 12.75-inch
                  (324mm) torpedo tubes Mk 32 (2x3).
                  AAW: NATO Sea Sparrow launcher Mk 29 (1x8, 16
                  reloads). 2 5-inch (127mm) Mk 45 (2x1); 2 Phalanx
                  CIWS being fitted.
                  SSM: 8 Harpoon missiles (2x4).
Sensors: *Surveillance:* SPS-40, SPS-55.
                  Fire Control: SPG-60, SPQ-9A, Mk 91.
                  Sonars: SQS-53.

The most controversial ships to be built for the US Navy since World War II,
the Spruance class was designed to replace the war-built destroyers of the
Gearing and Allen M. Sumner classes, which had undergone FRAM ASW
modification programmes during the 1960s but by the early 1970s were
nearing the end of their useful lives.

At 7,800t full load—more than twice the displacement of the destroyers it
was to replace—the *Spruance* epitomised the US Navy's design philosophy ▶

Below: *Oldendorf* **(DD-972) underway. The Spruance class are
now being fitted with canister launchers for Harpoon SSMs.**

▶of the 1970s. This philosophy envisaged the construction of large hulls with block superstructures which maximised internal volume, fitted out with machinery that could be easily maintained and, if necessary, replaced, and equipped with high-technology weapon systems that could be added to and updated by modular replacement at a later stage. The object was to minimise "platform" costs, which have no military pay-off, in favour of greater expenditure on weapon systems ("payload") in order to ensure that the ships would remain first-line units throughout the 30-year life-expectancy of their hulls.

In a further attempt to minimise "platform" costs the entire class was ordered from a single shipbuilder, the Litton/Ingalls Corporation, which invested heavily in a major production facility at Pascagoula, using advanced modular construction techniques.

The only "visible" weapons aboard *Spruance* when she was completed were 5-inch (127mm) Mk 45 lightweight gun mountings fore and aft and an ASROC box launcher forward of the bridge. In view of the size and cost of the ships this caused an immediate public outcry.

The advanced ASW qualities of the Spruance class are, however, largely hidden within the hull and the bulky superstructures. The ASROC launcher,

for example, has a magazine beneath it containing no less than 24 reloads. The large hangar to port of the after-funnel uptakes measures 49-54ft by 21-23ft (15-16.5m x 6.47m) and can accommodate two LAMPS helicopters. And to either side of the flight deck there are sliding doors in the hull which conceal triple Mk 32 torpedo tubes and torpedo-handling rooms.

Of even greater significance are the advanced submarine detection features of the class. The bow sonar is the new SQS-53, a solid-state improved version of the SQS-26, which can operate in a variety of active and passive modes, including direct path, bottom bounce and convergence zone. The SQS-53 has proved so successful that the SQS-35 VDS initially scheduled to be installed in these ships will not now be fitted. The adoption of an all-gas-turbine propulsion system, which employs paired LM2500 turbines *en echelon* in a unit arrangement, and which was selected partly because of the ease with which it can be maintained and because of its low ▶

Below: *Elliott* **(DD-967) underway. Gas-turbines give her rapid response and a low noise signature—a crucial factor in ASW operations. In the interests of fuel economy the ships generally trail one of their two shafts at cruise speed.**

▶manning requirements, has resulted in a significant reduction in underwater noise emission. The Spruance is therefore capable of near-silent ASW operations.

The class is also fitted with the latest computerised data systems in a well designed Combat Information Centre (CIC), and has the latest digital fire control systems—the Mk 86 GFCS and the Mk 116 underwater FC system.

Moreover, besides the weapon systems fitted on completion, the Spruance class was designed to accept a variety of other systems then at the development stage. Most ships have now received the Sea Sparrow Improved Point Defence Missile System (IPDMS), Harpoon anti-ship missiles (aft of the first funnel), and Whiskey-3 (WSC-3) satellite communications antennae. SLQ-32(V)2 ECM antennae are now being fitted, and provision has been made for the future replacement of the ASROC and Sea Sparrow launchers by Mk 26 launchers. Eventually these could be replaced by Ex 41 Vertical Launch Systems (VLS), each of which comprises a 29- or 61-missile box able to accommodate AAW, anti-ship, and ASW missiles. The Spruance class is scheduled to receive the SQR-19 TACTAS towed array when it becomes available.

The flexibility of the Spruance design is such that it has formed the basis both for the AAW destroyers originally ordered for Iran (see Kidd class) and of the new AEGIS cruiser (see Ticonderoga class).

One additional ship of the Spruance class was ordered in 1979. DD 997 was originally to have had increased hangar and flight-deck space for helicopter and VTOL operations, but it was a modification which found greater favour with Congress than with the US Navy, which has since decided to complete the ship to the standard Spruance configuration.

Above right: An early view of *Spruance* (DD-963) on sea trials in 1975. Note the layout of the funnels, which are en echelon.

Below: *Elliott* (DD-967) underway. Early criticism of the Spruance design has generally given way to praise.

Arthur W. Radford (DD-968).

Decatur

Completed:	1956-9.
Names:	DDG 31 *Decatur;* DDG 32 *John Paul Jones;* DDG 33 *Parsons;* DDG 34 *Somers.*
Displacement:	4,150t full load.
Dimensions:	418 oa x 45 x 20ft (127.5 x 13.8 x 6.1m).
Propulsion:	2-shaft geared steam turbines; 70,000shp = 32.5kts.
Armament:	*AAW:* single Mk 13 launcher (40) for Standard MR missiles; 1 5-inch (127mm) Mk 42.
	ASW: ASROC launcher Mk 16 (1x8); 6 12.75-inch (324mm) torpedo tubes Mk 32 (2x3).
	SSM: Harpoon missiles will be fired from Mk 13 launcher.
Sensors:	*Surveillance:* SPS-48, SPS-29E (SPS-40 in DDG 34), SPS-10B.
	Fire Control: 1 SPG-51C, 1 SPG-53B.
	Sonars: SQS-23.

These four ships were originally conventionally armed destroyers of the Forrest Sherman class. From 1965 until 1968 they underwent a major conversion to bring them up to a similar standard to the DDGs of the Charles F. Adams class.

The three-year refit included the removal of the after 5-inch (127mm) guns and their replacement by the Tartar missile system. A Mk 13 single-arm launcher together with its cylindrical magazine replaced the after gun mounting, and immediately forward of it a large deckhouse carrying a

single SPG-51 tracker/illuminator was constructed. Two massive lattice masts replaced the original tripods, giving the ships a distinctive profile. The purpose of the new mainmast was to carry the large SPS-48 3-D radar, which was just entering service. *Somers*, the last ship converted, also had her original SPS-29 air search radar replaced by an SPS-40. The initial conversion plan envisaged the operation of DASH anti-submarine drones, but when the DASH programme ran into problems, it was decided to fit an ASROC launcher instead.

It was originally intended that the entire Forrest Sherman class should undergo a similar conversion, but the cost of the programme proved to be prohibitive. Nor has the conversion proved to be particularly successful; the Decatur class suffers from excessive topweight, and although costly long-range detection and tracking facilities have been provided, the ships are limited to a single tracker/illuminator.

Top: *Parsons* (DDG-33). The single Mk 13 Tartar launcher is aft, with its SPG-51 FC radar mounted on a new deckhouse.

Above: A port bow view of *Somers* (DDG-34) underway off Hawaii. All four ships of the class serve in the Pacific.

Left: *John Paul Jones* (DDG-32) underway. These are the only US ships of their size to be fitted with the SPS-48 radar.

DDG

Charles F. Adams

Completed: 1960-4.
Names: DDG 2 *Charles F. Adams;* DDG 3 *John King;* DDG 4
Lawrence; DDG 5 *Claude V. Ricketts;* DDG 6 *Barney;*
DDG 7 *Henry B. Wilson;* DDG 8 *Lynde McCormick;*
DDG 9 *Towers;* DDG 10 *Sampson;* DDG 11 *Sellers;*
DDG 12 *Robison;* DDG 13 *Hoel;* DDG 14 *Buchanan;*
DDG 15 *Berkeley;* DDG 16 *Joseph Strauss;*
DDG 17 *Conyngham;* DDG 18 *Semmes;* DDG 19 *Tattnall;*
DDG 20 *Goldsborough;* DDG 21 *Cochrane;*
DDG 22 *Benjamin Stoddert;* DDG 23 *Richard E. Bird;*
DDG 24 *Waddell.*
Displacement: 3,370t standard; 4,500t full load.
Dimensions: 437 oa x 47 x 22ft (133.2 x 14.3 x 6.7m).
Propulsion: 2-shaft geared steam turbines; 70,000shp = 31.5kts.
Armament: *AAW:* twin Mk 11 launcher (42) *or* single Mk 13 launcher
(40) for Standard MR missiles; 2 5-inch (127mm)
Mk 42 (2x1).
ASW: ASROC launcher Mk 16 (1x8);
6 12.75-inch (324mm) torpedo tubes MK 32 (2x3).
SSM: Harpoon missiles from Mk 13 launcher.
Sensors: *Surveillance:* SPS-39, SPS-29/37 (DDG 2-14) *or*
SPS 40 (DDG-15-24), SPS-10C/D.
Fire Control: 2 SPG-51C, 1 SPG-53A/E/F.
Sonar: SQS-23.

The Charles F. Adams class is derived from the Forrest Sherman, with a Tartar launcher in place of the third 5-inch (127mm) gun mounting. It is still the standard AAW destroyer in service with the US Navy, and is employed together with the larger CGs to provide anti-air defence for the carrier battle groups.

The first 13 ships of the class were fitted with the twin-arm Mk 11 launcher but later ships have the single-arm Mk 13. The Mk 13 is a lightweight launcher with a high rate of fire—8 rounds per minute—which compensates in part for the single arm. Both launchers employ a cylindrical magazine containing two concentric rings of missiles. Overall length was increased by about 9m (29.5ft) to accommodate a Mk 16 ASROC launcher between the funnels. The installation of Tartar and ASROC made the *Charles F. Adams* one of the most formidably armed destroyers of its period, and the design was adopted by the Federal German and the Australian Navies.

In spite of their age these ships are still highly regarded in the US Navy. They have proved to be extremely useful, well balanced ships, whose only major defect has been their temperamental high-pressure boilers. In the late 1970s it was therefore proposed that they should undergo a major modernisation programme which would extend their service life beyond the nominal 30-year mark. Funding was to have been authorised in FY 1980-3 ▶

Below left: An aerial view of *Waddell* (DDG-24) underway in the Pacific. She has the single Mk 13 Tartar launcher aft.

Below: A DDG of the Charles F. Adams class in heavy weather. This unit has the older Mk 11 twin-arm Tartar launcher aft.

▶but it was feared that expenditure of this magnitude would adversely affect the programme of new construction, and the last ten ships will now receive a less fundamental modernisation.

Under the modernisation programme the original electronics will be given a complete overhaul and many new systems added. The SPS-39 3-D radar will be replaced by the SPS-52B, the SPS-29/37 by an SPS-40C, and the SPS-10 by an SPS-65. The original Gun Fire Control System (GFCS) will be replaced by the digital Mk 86, with SPG-60 and SPQ-9A antennae, and the NTDS will be updated, with provision of the SYS-1 integrated automatic detection and tracking system. An SQQ-23 PAIR active/passive sonar will replace the SQS-23, and ECM capabilities will be greatly enhanced by the installation of two SLQ-32(V)2 antennae. The modernisation will require at least 18 months per ship.

Twelve units of the class serve with the Pacific Fleet, and the remaining eleven in the Atlantic. It is envisaged that they will eventually be replaced by the DDGX now under development.

Richard E. Bird (DDG-23).

Right: Bow view of a DDG of the Charles F. Adams class. This unit has the SPS-40 air search radar on the foremast.

Below: *Henry B. Wilson* (DDG-7) underway in the Pacific. She has the twin-arm Mk 11 Tartar launcher aft.

Coontz

Completed: 1959-61.
Names: DDG 37 *Farragut;* DDG 38 *Luce;* DDG 39 *Macdonough;*
DDG 40 *Coontz;* DDG 41 *King;* DDG 42 *Mahan;*
DDG 43 *Dahlgren;* DDG 44 *Wm. V. Pratt;* DDG 45 *Dewey;*
DDG 46 *Preble.*
Displacement: 4,700t standard; 5,800t full load.
Dimensions: 513 oa x 53 x 25ft (156.2 x 15.9 x 7.6m).
Propulsion: 2-shaft geared steam turbines; 85,000shp = 33kts.
Armament: *AAW:* twin Mk 10 launcher (40) for Standard ER missiles;
1 5-inch (127mm) Mk 42.
ASW: ASROC launcher Mk 16 (1x8); 6 12.75-inch
(324mm) torpedo tubes Mk 32 (2x3).
SSM: 8 Harpoon missiles (2x4).
Sensors: *Surveillance:* SPS-48 (SPS-49 in DDG 43, 46),
SPS-29/37, SPS-10.
Fire Control: 2 SPG-55B, 1 SPG-53A.
Sonars: SQS-23.

The ten ships of the Coontz class constitute the first group of AAW "frigates"
completed for the US Navy during the 1960s. Unlike the later ships of the
Leahy and Belknap classes they have a flush-decked hull, and this feature,
together with their twin lattice mast/funnel arrangement, reveals their
derivation from the all-gun DLs of the early 1950s. They also have much
lower endurance than later ships, and this factor appears to have been
largely responsible for their redesignation as DDGs in 1975 (the Leahy and
Belknap classes became CGs). They nevertheless carry a similar armament
to the later ships, have been brought up to the same standard as regards
electronics, and perform an identical mission in defence of the carrier battle
groups which are described and shown on pages 10-13. ▶

Above: The destroyer *Luce* (DDG-38) seen here in the
Mediterranean. These ships were formerly classified as DLG.

Below: *Macdonough* (DDG-39). She and her sister ships underwent a major AAW modernisation programme in the early 1970s.

▶ The *Coontz* has a twin Mk 10 launcher aft, a single 5-inch (127mm) gun forward, an ASROC box launcher above it in "B" position, and triple anti-submarine tubes amidships. From 1968 until 1976 the class underwent a major modernisation similar to that of the *Leahy*. The SPS-39 3-D radar was replaced by an SPS-48, the Terrier guidance system was changed from command (employing SPG-49 radars) to semi-active guidance (employing the SPG-55), and a computer-based NTDS was installed – *Mahan* and *King*, which had been trials ships for the system 1961-2, had theirs updated. *Farragut* had her ASW capability enhanced by the provision of a reloading magazine for ASROC at the forward end of the superstructure, but she

remained the only ship thus fitted. All ships had the original 3-inch (76mm) AA guns removed, and these were later replaced by Harpoon. In 1979 *Mahan* received the SM-2 missile, and this will eventually be fitted to the rest of the class. They are also scheduled to receive the SQQ-23 PAIR sonar, but will not be fitted with Phalanx.

All except *Preble* currently serve in the Atlantic, where their limited endurance is of less consequence than in the broader reaches of the Pacific.

Below: The destroyer *Coontz* (DDG-40) underway. She established the armament pattern for the US Navy's carrier escorts.

DD
Forrest Sherman

Completed: 1955-9.
Names: DD 931 *Forrest Sherman;* DD 942 *Bigelow;*
DD 944 *Mullinix;* DD 945 *Hull;* DD 946 *Edson* (NRF).
DD 951 *Turner Joy.* (ASW conversions). DD 933 *Barry;*
DD 937 *Davis;* DD 938 *Jonas Ingram;* DD 940 Manley;
DD 941 *Du Pont;* DD 943 *Blandy;* DD 948 *Morton;*
DD 950 *Richard S. Edwards.*
Displacement: 2,800t standard, 4,050t full load.
Dimensions: 418 oa x 45 x 22ft (127.5 x 13.7 x 6.7m).
Propulsion: 2-shaft geared steam turbines; 70,00shp = 32.5kts.
Armament: (Unmodified units) *ASW:* 6 12.75-inch (324mm) torpedo
tubes Mk 32 (2x3).
AAW: 3 5-inch (127mm) Mk 42 (3x1).
(ASW Conversions). *ASW:* ASROC launcher Mk 16 (1x8);
6 12.75-inch (324mm) torpedo tubes Mk 32 (2x3).
AAW: 2 5-inch (127mm) Mk 42.
Sensors: *Surveillance:* SPS-37 or SPS-40, SPS-10.
Fire Control: SPG-53.
Sonars: SQS-23, SQS-35 IVDS in ASW-modified ships.

The Forest Sherman class were the first postwar US destroyers. Although
conventionally armed, they followed current tactical thinking in abandoning
anti-ship torpedoes, which were replaced by four fixed 21-inch (533mm)
"long" ASW torpedoes, and in mounting a lesser number of guns with higher
performance than those of their war-built predecessors.

The conventional armament was quickly overtaken by new technological
developments––in particular the advent of the nuclear submarine and the
surface-to-air missile–and an extensive conversion programme was drawn
up. Four ships were given the Tartar missile system (see Decatur class) but
the cost of the conversion precluded its extension to the rest of the class.
Eight ships were therefore given a limited ASW conversion between 1967
and 1971. The second gun mounting was replaced by an ASROC launcher
and the fixed A/S tubes by triple Mk 32 trainable tubes; surveillance radars
were updated and an independent variable depth sonar fitted above the
stern.

Even this limited conversion programme ran into cost problems, and the remaining six ships of the class received only those modifications which entailed a minimum of structural alterations. They retained all three 5-inch (127mm) guns and were not fitted with ASROC or VDS.

From 1975 onwards *Hull* served as trial ship for the 8-inch (205mm) Mk 71 Major Calibre Light Weight Gun (MCLWG). The mounting replaced the forward gun until 1979, when it was removed. *Edson* is now in reserve, but it is anticipated that the other units will remain active for some years yet.

Below left: The destroyer *Forrest Sherman* (DD-931) underway. She retains her original configuration with three 5-inch guns.

Below: An aerial view of an ASW conversion of the Forest Sherman class, showing clearly the ASROC launcher aft.

Frigates

FFG

Oliver Hazard Perry

Completed: 1977 onwards.
Names: FFG 7 *Oliver H. Perry;* FFG 8 *McInerney;*
FFG 9 *Wadsworth;* FFG 10 *Duncan;* FFG 11 *Clark;*
FFG 12 *George Philip;* FFG 13 *Samuel E. Morison;*
FFG 14 *Sides;* FFG 15 *Estocin;* FFG 16 *Clifton Sprague;*
FFG 19 *John A. Moore;* FFG 20 *Antrim;* FFG 21 *Flatley;*
FFG 22 *Fahrion;* FFG 23 *Lewis B. Puller;*
FFG 24 *Jack Williams;* FFG 25 *Copeland;* FFG 26 *Gallery;*
FFG 27 *Mahlon S. Tisdale;* FFG 28 *Boone;*
FFG 29 *Stephen W. Groves;* FFG 30 *Reid;* FFG 31 *Stark;*
FFG 32 *John L. Hall;* + 22 building.
Displacement: 3,710t full load.
Dimensions: 445 oa x 45 x 25ft (135.6 x 13.7 x 7.5m).
Propulsion: 1-shaft COGAG; 2 LM2500 gas turbines;
40,000bhp = 28kts.
Armament: *AAW:* single Mk 13 launcher (40) for Standard MR missiles;
1 76mm (3-inch) Mk 75; 1 Phalanx CIWS being fitted.
ASW: 2 LAMPS helicopters; 6 12.75-inch (324mm)
torpedo tubes Mk 32 (2x3).
SSM: Harpoon missiles from Mk 13 launcher.
Sensors: *Surveillance:* SPS-49, SPS-55.
Fire Control: STIR (modified SPG-60).
Sonars: SQS-26.

The FFG 7 design has its origins in the Patrol Frigate first proposed in September 1970. The latter was to constitute the "low" end of the so-called "high/low" mix, providing large numbers of cheap second-rate escorts with reduced capabilities to counterbalance the sophisticated but costly specialist ASW and AAW vessels whose primary mission was to protect the carriers. Strict limitations were therefore imposed on cost, displacement and manpower requirements.

Unlike its near-contemporary, the high-value *Spruance,* which had its own specialised production facility, the FFG 7 was designed to be built anywhere. Simple construction techniques were encouraged, making maximum use of flat panels and bulkheads, and passageways are generally straight. The hull structure can be prefabricated in modules of 35, 100, 200 or 400 tons, allowing the various shipyards to use the most convenient size. As a result the programme is running well to schedule with some units being delivered early, and costs have been kept remarkably close to the original estimates.

The application of the USAF-derived "fly-before-buy" concept to the FFG 7 programme has meant a two-year gap between the completion of the first ship and the rest of the class, making it possible to iron out any problems▶

Right: *Oliver Hazard Perry* **(FFG-7) underway. The single Mk 13 Tartar launcher is visible on the forecastle.**

The US frigate is essentially a cheap, 2nd-rate type designed to escort convoys and groups of amphibious ships. One-shaft operation and a modest speed are therefore acceptable, although good endurance is essential. As with destroyers, some frigates are configured for air defence (FFG) while others are primarily for ASW (FF). The latest ships of the Oliver Hazard Perry class can perform both missions. They will be succeeded in FY 1983 by a new design known as the FFGX.

experienced during trials with the first ship, and to incorporate any necessary modifications into the following units while building. Moreover, before even the lead ship had been completed, the individual systems with which she was to be equipped had already been tested on ships of other classes.

Like the frigates which preceded her, the *Oliver Hazard Perry* has a "second-class" propulsion plant on one screw. The layout is, however, much more compact than that of the *Knox* as a result of the adoption of gas turbines. Two LM2500s – the same model as that installed in the *Spruance* – are located side-by-side in a single engine room. Two small retractable

propulsion pods fitted just aft of the sonar dome provide back-up during docking procedures, and these can drive the ship at 6 knots in an emergency.

The balance of the armament is more closely oriented to AAW than that of the *Knox*, which was a specialist ASW design. The FFG 7 has a Mk 13 launcher forward for Standard MR surface-to-air missiles and Harpoon anti-ship missiles, and an OTO-Melara 76mm (3-inch) quick-firing gun atop the▶

Below: ***Oliver Hazard Perry*** **(FFG-7) is the first of the new Patrol Frigates. Large numbers are under construction.**

▶bulky superstructure block. ASROC has been abandoned altogether, but there is a broad hangar aft for two LAMPS helicopters. The sonar, which is hull-mounted inside a rubber dome, is a new austere type which has neither the long range nor the multi-mode capability of the SQS-26 fitted to previous frigates. It is, however, envisaged that the FFG 7 would operate in conjunction with other frigates equipped with the SQS-26 and would receive target information from their sonars via data links.

Whereas the *Spruance* was designed to incorporate a large amount of space for future growth, the FFG 7 has been strictly tailored to accommodate only those systems envisaged in the near future. These include the SH-60 Seahawk LAMPS III (together with its RAST recovery system), the SQR-19 tactical towed array, fin stabilisers, a Link 11 data transfer system, and a single Phalanx CIWS gun. These items alone represent a lot of growth. Once these modifications have been made, however, there remains only a 50-ton margin for further growth, and if any additional items of equipment are to be fitted, others will have to be removed.

Right: *Oliver Hazard Perry* **(FFG-7). The surveillance radar is the new SPS-49, which replaces the SPS 37/43 series.**

Below: *Oliver Hazard Perry* **(FFG-7) on sea trials. Note the large double hangar and the short, stubby funnel.**

Knox

Completed: 1969-74.

Names:
FF 1052 *Knox;* FF 1053 *Roark;* FF 1054 *Gray;*
FF 1055 *Hepburn;* FF 1056 *Connole;* FF 1057 *Rathburne;*
FF 1058 *Meyerkord;* FF 1059 *W.S. Sims;* FF 1060 *Lang;*
FF 1061 *Patterson;* FF 1062 *Whipple;* FF 1063 *Reasoner;*
FF 1064 *Lockwood;* FF 1065 *Stein;*
FF 1066 *Marvin Shields;* FF 1067 *Francis Hammond;*
FF 1068 *Vreeland;* FF 1069 *Bagley;* FF 1070 *Downes;*
FF 1071 *Badger;* FF 1072 *Blakely;*
FF 1073 *Robert E. Peary;* FF 1074 *Harold E. Holt;*
FF 1075 *Trippe;* FF 1076 *Fanning;* FF 1077 *Ouellet;*
FF 1078 *Joseph Hewes;* FF 1079 *Bowen;* FF 1080 *Paul;*
FF 1081 *Aylwin;* FF 1082 *Elmer Montgomery;*
FF 1083 *Cook;* FF 1084 *McCandless;*
FF 1085 *Donald B. Beary;* FF 1086 *Brewton;*
FF 1087 *Kirk;* FF 1088 *Barbey;* FF 1089 *Jesse L. Brown;*
FF 1090 *Ainsworth;* FF 1091 *Miller;*
FF 1091 *Miller;* FF 1092 *Thomas C. Hart;*
FF 1093 *Capodanno;* FF 1094 *Pharris;* FF 1095 *Truett;*
FF 1096 *Valdez;* FF 1097 *Moinester.*

Displacement: 3,011t standard; 4,100t full load.

Dimensions: 438 oa x 47 x 25ft (133.5 x 14.3 x 7.6m).

Propulsion: 1-shaft geared steam turbines; 35,000shp = 27kts.

Armament:
ASW: ASROC launcher Mk 16 (1x8, reloadable);
1 SH-2F helicopter; 4 12.75-inch (324mm) torpedo
tubes Mk 32 (4x1).
AAW: BPDMS launcher Mk 25 (1x8) in 31 ships;
1 5-inch (127mm) Mk 42.
SSM: Harpoon missiles from ASROC Launcher.

Sensors:
Surveillance: SPS-40, SPS-10.
Fire Control: SPG-53A/D/F, Mk 115.
Sonars: SQS-26CX, SQS-35 IVDS in some ships.

The Knox class began as a Design Work Study of the Brooke-class missile escort. Congressional opposition to the mounting costs of fitting escorts with the Tartar system resulted, however, in the abandonment of the latter class after only six units had been laid down, The *Knox* was therefore redesigned as an ASW Escort. ▶

Above: A bow view of *Moinester* (FF-1097), the last ship of the Knox class. The ASROC launcher is visible behind the 5-inch gun.

Below left: *Joseph L. Hewes* (FF-1078) soon after completion. The helicopter platform and hangar have yet to be modified.

Below: An aerial view of *Stein* (FF-1065) in the Pacific. Note the enlarged helicopter platform and the telescopic hangar.

Although the *Knox* retained the one-shaft propulsion system of the Garcia/Brooke design, the complex pressure-fired boilers of the latter were abandoned in favour of a "safer", more conventional steam plant. This necessitated an increase in size without creating any extra space for weapons.

Originally the two 5-inch (127mm) Mk 38 guns of the *Garcia* were to have been replaced by a combination of a single 5-inch Mk 42 and the ill-fated Sea Mauler point-defence missile. The Sea Mauler was eventually replaced by the Sea Sparrow BPDMS–a system not contemplated when the *Knox* was designed.

Other "hiccups" in the development of the *Knox* include the abandonment of a fixed "billboard" ECM antenna which influenced the design of the tall mack, of the pair of fixed torpedo tubes (for Mk 37/Mk 48 torpedoes) which were to have been fitted in the stern, and of the DASH programme.

Ultimately the abandonment of DASH worked to the ships' advantage, as it was replaced by the LAMPS I manned helicopter. As with the previous two classes of escort, the hangar received a telescopic extension, giving overall dimensions of 42-47ft by 15-18ft (12.6-14.3m x 4.4-5.6m). Taken together

with the reloadable ASROC launcher and the SQS-26 sonar, this gave the *Knox* a first-class anti-submarine outfit, which rescued the design from an unpromising beginning.

Besides the Sea Sparrow BPDMS, many ships have received the SQS-35 independent variable depth sonar since completion. All will receive the SQR-18 towed array in the near future. Most ships have now had their ASROC launchers modified to fire Harpoon, and it is planned to replace Sea Sparrow with a single Phalanx CIWS mounting.

In spite of the early problems experienced the *Knox* has become one of the most useful and versatile classes of US warship. It is also the largest class of major combatants completed in the West in the postwar era, and would have been larger still but for the cancellation of ten ships authorised in FY 1968 to finance other programmes.

Below: The frigate *Connole* (FF-1056) underway in the Atlantic. The Knox class is now being fitted with bow bulwarks in order to improve sea-keeping. The class has proved successful in service, despite initial criticism of the design.

Brooke

Completed: 1966-8.
Names: FFG 1 *Brooke;* FFG 2 *Ramsey;* FFG 3 *Schofield;*
FFG 4 *Talbot;* FFG 5 *Richard L. Page;* FFG 6 *Julius A. Furer.*
Displacement: 2,640t standard; 3,245t full load.
Dimensions: 415 oa x 44 x 24ft (126.3 x 13.5 x 7.3m).
Propulsion: 1-shaft geared steam turbine; 35,000shp = 27kts.
Armament: *AAW:* single Mk 22 launcher (16) for Standard MR missiles;
1 5-inch (127mm) Mk 30.
ASW: ASROC launcher Mk 16 (reloadable in FFG 4-6);
1 SH-2F helicopter; 6 12.75-inch (324mm) torpedo
tubes Mk 32 (2x3).
Sensors: *Surveillance:* SPS-52D, SPS-10F.
Fire Control: 1 SPG-51C, Mk35.
Sonars: SQS-26AX.

The Brooke class is a Tartar modification of the Garcia class of ASW escorts.
The two classes share the same basic hull, single-shaft propulsion plant, and
general layout, but the *Brooke* has a single Mk 22 Tartar launcher in place of
the second 5-inch (127mm) Mk 30 of the *Garcia.*

The Mk 22 launcher has a single-ring magazine with a much-reduced capacity of 16 rounds compared with the 40-round installation which is standard to larger vessels. The above-water sensor outfit is also comparatively austere; there is an SPS-52 3-D radar but no independent air search antenna, and only a single SPG-51 tracker/illuminator. In spite of this Congress baulked at the $11m increase in cost compared with the gun-armed *Garcia*, and rejected the proposal for a further 10 units in FY 1964.

Since completion, the Brooke class has undergone similar modifications to the Garcia. The two Mk 25 torpedo tubes initially incorporated in the stern have been removed and, following the abandonment of the DASH programme, the hangar has been enlarged and fitted with a telescopic extension to accommodate a LAMPS helicopter. Overall hangar dimensions are now 40-52ft by 15-17ft (12-15.8m x 4.4-5.1m).

In 1974 *Talbot* was refitted to evaluate various systems which were to be installed in the FFG 7, including the OTO Melara 76mm gun, the Mk 92 and STIR fire control systems, and the SQS-56 sonar. She has since reverted to her original configuration.

Below: *Julius A. Furer* **(FFG-6). The sloping bridge-face conceals an ASROC reload magazine, fitted only in the last three ships of the class. The single Mk 16 Tartar launcher and its SPG-51 FC radar are amidships, just forward of the helicopter hangar.**

Garcia

Completed: 1964-68.
Names: FF 1040 *Garcia;* FF 1041 *Bradley;*
FF 1043 *Edward McDonnell;* FF 1044 *Brumby;*
FF 1045 *Davidson;* FF 1047 *Voge;* FF 1048 *Sample;*
FF 1049 *Koelsch;* FF 1050 *Albert David;* FF 1051 *O'Callahan.*
Displacement: 2,620t standard; 3,400t full load.
Dimensions: 415 oa x 44 x 24ft (126.3 x 13.5 x 7.3m).
Propulsion: 1-shaft geared steam turbine; 35,000shp = 27kts.
Armament: *ASW:* ASROC launcher Mk 16 (1x8) reloadable in FFG
(1047-51). 1 SH-2F helicopter (except FF 1048, 1050)
6 12.75-inch (324mm) torpedo tubes Mk 32 (2x3).
AAW: 2 5-inch (127mm) Mk 30 (2x1).
Sensors: *Surveillance:* SPS-40, SPS-10.
Fire Control: Mk 35.
Sonars: SQS-26AXR (FF 1040-45) *or*
SQS-26BX (FF 1047-51), SQR-15 TASS
(FF 1048, 1050 only).

The Garcia-class ocean escort was evolved from the Bronstein design which, although similar in size to contemporary European escorts, proved too small for the US Navy. Improvements included a larger, flush-decked hull, a heavier gun armament, and the provision of a hangar aft for DASH anti-submarine drones. The last five units were also given a reload magazine for ASROC at the forward end of the bridge, which has a distinctive sloping face in these ships. The earlier units were initially fitted with two stern tubes for Mk 25 torpedoes, but these have now been removed.

Only *Bradley* is thought to have operated DASH before the programme was abandoned. All except *Sample* and *Albert David* (which are fitted instead with a towed array) subsequently had their hangars enlarged and a

telescopic extension fitted to enable them to operate manned LAMPS helicopters. This modification has brought with it a significant increase in ASW capabilities.

A compact one-shaft steam propulsion plant employing pressure-fired boilers was adopted to maximise the internal volume available for weapons and electronics. The pressure-fired boilers proved complex to operate and maintain, however, and concern about the reliability of such a high-technology system—especially in a ship with only a single shaft—led to a reversion to conventional boilers in the succeeding Knox class.

Below: Stern view of a frigate of the Garcia class. Note the helicopter hangar, which now has a telescopic extension.

Bottom: The frigate _Voge_ (FF-1047) comes alongside the carrier _America_ (CV-66). The second 5-inch gun is visible amidships.

FF
Bronstein

Completed: 1963.
Names: FF 1037 *Bronstein;* FF 1038 *McCloy.*
Displacement: 2,360t standard; 2,650t full load.
Dimensions: 372 oa x 41 x 23ft (113.2 x 12.3 x 7m).
Propulsion: 1-shaft geared steam turbine; 20,000shp = 24kts.
Armament: *ASW:* ASROC launcher Mk 16 (1x8);
6 12.75-inch (324mm) torpedo tubes Mk 32 (2x3).
AAW: 2 3-inch (76mm) Mk 33 (1x2).
Sensors: *Surveillance:* SPS-40, SPS-10.
Fire Control: Mk 35.
Sonars: SQS-26, SQR-15 TASS.

The development of high-speed nuclear-powered submarines by the Soviet Union in the late 1950s effectively outdated even those US Navy DEs which were under construction at that time. The US Navy responded by designing a new type of ocean escort radically different from its predecessors in every respect. The result was the two ships of the Bronstein class.

Steam propulsion was adopted in place of the traditional diesels, although, contrary to European practice, the single shaft of the DE was retained. The most revolutionary feature of the design, however, was that the entire ship was built around a first-class ASW outfit comprising the latest weapons and sensors. The slim, tapered bow conceals a massive SQS-26 sonar dome, which was originally to be matched with the ASROC anti-submarine missile and a DASH drone, for which a flight deck was provided immediately abaft the superstructure. When DASH was cancelled, however, the superstructure arrangement proved too cramped to fit a hangar large enough to take a LAMPS helicopter, and only ASROC and the triple Mk 32 tubes remain.

The gun armament was on a par with previous DEs. A third 3-inch (76mm) gun on the low quarterdeck was removed in the mid-1970s to make room for a large towed array. The superstructure comprises a single compact block surmounted by a tall mack carrying the air search radar and ECM aerials.

Although unsatisfactory in some respects, these two ships set the pattern for all ocean escorts built for the US Navy over the next two decades.

Above: Bow view of a Bronstein-class frigate. Later frigates have a single 5-inch gun in place of the twin 3-inch mounting.

Below left: The frigate *Bronstein* (FF-1037) underway. This ship was the first of a series of large ocean-going escorts.

Below: *McCloy* (FF-1038), showing the large helicopter deck from which DASH antisubmarine drones were to have been operated.

Patrol Combatants

Pegasus

Completed: 1977-82.
Names: PHM 1 *Pegasus;* PHM 2 *Hercules;* PHM 3 *Taurus;*
PHM 4 *Aquila;* PHM 5 *Aries;* PHM 6 *Gemini.*
Displacement: 231t full load.
Dimensions: 132 x 28 x 6ft (40 x 8.0 x 1.9m).
Propulsion: (hullborne) 2 Mercedes-Benz diesels; 1600bhp = 12kts.
(foilborne) 1 General Electric gas-turbine;
18,000bhp = 40kts.
Armament: 8 Harpoon (2x4); 1 3-inch (76mm) Mk 75.
Sensors: *Fire Control:* 1 Mk 92 (Mk 94 in PHM 1).

The PHM was one of the four new designs in the "low" programme advocated in Zumalt's Project 60 (see Introduction). It was envisaged that squadrons of these fast patrol craft would be deployed at the various choke-points—in particular those in the Mediterranean and the NW Pacific—through which the surface units of the Soviet Navy needed to pass in order to reach open waters. High speed and a heavy armament of anti-ship missiles would enable the PHM to make rapid interceptions, and the relatively low unit cost meant that large numbers could be bought.

The US Navy has traditionally shown little interest in small patrol craft, and has concentrated on ocean-going construction to meet its maritime commitments. Seventeen gas-turbine-powered gunboats (PG) were built in the mid-1960s to counter Cuban-inspired insurgency in the Caribbean, and these saw extensive employment in Vietnam. Only two remain in service, and they are used only for training. The six missile hydrofoils of the Pegasus class are all that remain of 30 planned in the 1970s.

The Italian and Federal German Navies, with similar requirements in the Mediterranean and the Baltic respectively, participated in the development of the design. The Germans planned to build 12 units of their own in addition to the 30 originally projected for the US Navy.

Technical problems with the hydrofoil system resulted in cost increases, and opponents of the PHM programme, pointing to the limited capabilities of the design, tried to obtain cancellation of all except the lead vessel. Congress insisted, however, on the construction of the six units for which funds had already been authorised.

The propulsion system of the PHM comprises separate diesels driving two waterjets for hullborne operation and a single gas turbine for high-speed foilborne operation.

In order to fit in with the requirements of the NATO navies the OTO-Melara 76mm gun and a Dutch fire control system were adopted. The Mk 94 GFCS on *Pegasus* was bought direct from HSA but the Mk 92 systems on the other five are being manufactured under licence. The original anti-ship missile armament has been doubled, with two quadruple mounts replacing the four singles first envisaged.

Below: *Pegasus* **(PHM-1) at speed. She can make 40 knots on her foils. She is exceptionally well-armed for a vessel of her size, with quadruple canisters of Harpoon antiship missiles aft and an OTO-Melara 76mm (3-inch) automatic gun forward.**

Amphibious Warfare Vessels

LCC
Blue Ridge

Completed: 1970-71
Names: LCC 19 *Blue Ridge;* LCC 20 *Mount Whitney.*
Displacement: 19,290t full load.
Dimensions: 620 oa x 82 wl, 108 upper deck x 27ft.
(188.5 x 25.3, 33 x 8.2m).
Propulsion: 1-shaft steam turbine; 22,000shp = 20kts.
Armament: 2 BPDMS launchers Mk 25
4 3-inch (76mm) Mk 33 (2x2).
Sensors: *Surveillance:* SPS-48, SPS-40, SPS-10.
Fire Control: 2 Mk 115, 2 Mk 35.

These two vessels were built to provide specialised command facilities for the amphibious fleets in the Pacific and Atlantic respectively. They replaced the more numerous war-built AGFs, which had inadequate speed for the new 20-knot amphibious squadrons. The basic design is that of the Iwo Jima-class LPH, with the former hangar occupied by command spaces, offices and accommodation. Prominent sponsons for LCPLs and ships' boats project from the sides, and the broad flat upper deck is lined with a variety of surveillance, ECM/ESM and communications aerials. The LCCs

The bulk of the US Navy's Amphibious fleet was built in the late 1950s and the 1960s. It comprises ships for vertical assault employing helicopters (LHPs), and others for the landing of troops, vehicles and stores via landing craft (LPDs/LSDs) or by direct beaching (LSTs). In the 1970s a new class incorporating all but the last of these functions (the LHA) was completed. The oldest LSDs will be replaced by a new design (LSD-41), while the LPHs will be replaced by amphibious transport docks (LHDs)

---

are fitted with the Naval Tactical Data System (NTDS), the Amphibious Command Information System (ACIS) and the Naval Intelligence Processing System (NIPS). As completed, they had only two twin 3-inch (76mm) mountings for defence against aircraft, but two BPDMS launchers were added in 1974. Two utility helicopters are generally operated from the flight pad aft but there are no hangar or maintenance facilities.

The command facilities originally provided for a naval Commander Amphibious Task Group (CATG), a Marine Landing Force Commander (LFC), Air Control Group Commander, and their respective staffs, with accommodation for up to 200 officers and 500 enlisted men in addition to the 780-man crew.

There were plans for a third ship (AGC 21), which would have provided both fleet command and amphibious command facilities, but inadequate speed for fleet work was an important factor in her cancellation. With the demise of the Cleveland-class CGs fleet flagships in the late 1970s, however, *Blue Ridge* and *Mount Whitney* became flagships of the Seventh (W. Pacific) and the Second (Atlantic) Fleets respectively.

Below left: The Amphibious Command Ship *Blue Ridge* (LCC-19) off Hawaii. She now serves as flagship of the US 7th Fleet.

Below: An aerial view of *Blue Ridge*. The flat upper deck carries a variety of communications aerials.

Tarawa

Completed: 1976-80.
Names: LHA 1 *Tarawa;* LHA 2 *Saipan;* LHA 3 *Belleau Wood;* LHA 4 *Nassau;* LHA 5 *Peleliu.*
Displacement: 39,300t full load.
Dimensions: 820 oa × 107 wl 126 flight deck × 26ft (249 9 × 32.5, 38.4 × 7.9m)
Propulsion: 2-shaft geared steam turbines; 70,000shp = 24kts.
Armament: 2 BPDMS launchers Mk 25 (2x8); 3 5-inch (127mm) Mk 45 (3x1); 6 20mm (6x1).
Aircraft: 30 helicopters (CH-46D, CH-53D/E, AH-1T, UH-1N).
Troops: 2,000.
Landing-craft: 4 LCU, 2 LCM.
Sensors: *Surveillance:* SPS-52B, SPS-40B, SPS-10F.
Fire Control: SPG-60, SPQ-9A, 2 Mk 115.

The last in a series of ocean-going amphibious vessels ordered during the 1960s, the Tarawa-class LHAs were to combine in a single hull capabilities which had previously required a number of separate specialist types—the

LPH, the LSD, the LPD, the LCC and the LKA (see following entries). The result is a truly massive ship with more than twice the displacement of any previous amphibious unit and with dimensions approaching those of a conventional aircraft carrier. Nine ships were originally projected, to be constructed by means of advanced modular techniques at the same Litton/Ingalls yard that built the Spruance-class destroyers. In 1971, however, with the Vietnam War drawing to a close, the order was reduced to five, resulting in some financial penalties.

The increase in size of these ships is a direct consequence of the need to provide a helicopter hangar *and* a docking-well. The hangar is located directly above the docking-well; both are 268ft in length and 78ft wide (81.6 x 23.7m), and the hangar has a 20ft (6.5m) overhead to enable the latest heavy-lift helicopters to be accommodated. In order to maximise internal capacity the ship's sides are vertical for two-thirds of its length. Hangar capacity is greater than that of the Iwo Jima class, and all the helicopters can be struck down if necessary. The customary loading would include about 12 CH-46D Sea Knights, six of the larger CH-53D Sea Stallions, four AH1▶

Below: *Tarawa* (LHA-1), displaying her massive flight deck. Note the vertical sides of the hull, which testify to the presence of a capacious docking well in the after part of the ship.

▶SeaCobra gunships, and a couple of UH-1N utility helicopters. The Pacific-based ships have operated AV-8 Harriers and have their flight decks marked out accordingly. The flight deck is served by a side lift to port and a larger centre-line lift set into the stern. The latter can handle the new CH-53E Super Stallion heavy lift helicopter.

The docking-well can accommodate four of the big LCUs, which can each lift three M-48 or M-60 tanks, or 150 tons of cargo. Two LCM-6 landing-craft, which can each carry 80 troops or 34 tons of cargo, are stowed immediately aft of the island and are handled by a large crane. The docking-well is divided into two by a central support structure incorporating a conveyor belt, which runs forward onto the vehicle decks. The conveyor belt is served by a group of three cargo elevators at its forward end, and by a further two elevators in the docking-well area. The elevators bring supplies for the landing force, stored in pallets each weighing approximately one ton, up from the cargo holds deep in the ship. The pallets are transferred to the

landing-craft by one of 11 monorail cars which work overhead in the welldeck area. The after pair of elevators can also lift pallets directly to the hangar deck, where they are loaded onto transporters. An angled ramp leads from the hangar deck to the forward end of the island, enabling the transfer of pallets to the flight deck for loading onto the helicopters.

Forward of the docking-well are the vehicle decks, interconnected by a series of ramps and able to accommodate some 200 vehicles. Tanks, artillery and trucks are generally stowed at the forward end, and up to 40 LVTP-7 amphibious personnel carriers, each with a capacity of 25 troops, can be accommodated. Eight LVTPs can be launched from the welldeck simultaneously with the four big LCUs. ▶

Below: *Tarawa* underway in the Gulf of Mexico. Two CH-46 Sea Knight helicopters are positioned on the flight deck, with another landing on. Note the side lift to port.

▶ Above the vehicle decks is the accommodation deck, with berths for some 2,000 troops in addition to the 900 crew. At the forward end there is a combined acclimatisation room/gymnasium, in which humidity and temperature can be controlled to simulate the climate in which the troops will be operating. At the after end there is a large, well equipped hospital, which can if necessary expand into accommodation spaces. Separate personnel elevators serve the hospital and the accommodation area, enabling rapid transfers to and from the flight deck.

The large block superstructure houses extensive command facilities, with accommodation for both the Commander Amphibious Task Group (CATG) and the Landing Force Commander (LFC) and their respective staffs. To enable these officers to exercise full tactical control over amphibious operations the LHAs are provided with a computer-based Integrated Tactical Amphibious Warfare. Data System (ITAWDS), which keeps track of the position of troops, helicopters, vehicles, landing-craft and cargo after they leave the ship. The system also tracks the position of designated targets ashore, and aims and fires the ship's armament, which is orientated towards fire support and short-range anti-aircraft defence.

The versatility of the LHAs enables them to combine with any of the other amphibious types in the US Navy inventory. A typical PhibRon deployment would combine an LHA with an LPD and one/two LSTs. The only major limitation of the design appears to be the inability to accommodate more than one of the new air-cushion landing-craft (AALC) because of the layout of the docking-well.

Right: *Nassau* **(LHA-4) running sea trials in 1979. Vehicles can transfer from the hangar area to the flight deck via ramps.**

Below: The stern of an LHA of the Tarawa class. The heavy stern doors give access to the large docking well.

Tarawa (LHA-1).

Iwo Jima

Completed: 1961-70.
Names: LPH 2 *Iwo Jima;* LPH 3 *Okinawa;* LPH 7 *Guadalcanal;*
LPH 9 *Guam;* LPH 10 *Tripoli;* LPH 11 *New Orleans;*
LPH 12 *Inchon.*
Displacement: 17,000t light; 18,300t full load.
Dimensions: 592 oa x 84 wl, 112 flight deck x 26ft
(180 x 25.6, 34.1 x 7.9m).
Propulsion: 1-shaft geared steam turbine; 22,000shp = 20kts.
Armament: 2 BPDMS launchers Mk 25 (2x8); 4 3-inch
(76mm) Mk 33 (2x2).
Aircraft: 25 helicopters (CH-46D, CH-53D, AH-1T, UH-1N).
Sensors: *Surveillance:* SPS-40, SPS-10.
Fire Control: 2 Mk 115.

The US Marine Corps had initiated experiments in helicopter assault
techniques as early as 1948, and in 1955 the former escort carrier *Thetis
Bay* underwent a major conversion to test the "vertical envelopment"
concept. Two years later the escort carrier *Block Island* was taken in hand
for a similar conversion, but this was halted as an economy measure. The
concept proved such a success, however, that the Navy embarked on a
programme of new purpose-built helicopter carriers, which became the Iwo
Jima class. As an interim measure three Essex-class carriers were modified
for helicopter operations and reclassified as amphibious assault ships. These
and the converted escort carriers took the "missing" LPH numbers in the
series until their demise in the late 1960s.

As the ships of the Iwo Jima class were amphibious—not fleet—units, many
of the refinements associated with first-line vessels were dispensed with in
the interests of economy. The design was based on a mercantile hull with a
one-shaft propulsion system capable of a sustained 20 knots. A large central
box hangar was adopted with 20ft (6.5m) clearance, a capacity of about 20
helicopters, and with side lifts disposed *en echelon* at either end. The lifts,
50ft x 34ft (15.2 x 10.4m) and with a capacity of 44-50,000lb (20-
22,725kg), can be folded upwards to close the hangar openings. Fore and
aft of the hangar there is accommodation for a Marine battalion, and the
ships have a well equipped hospital with 300 beds. ▶

Right: *Tripoli* **(LPH-10) entering Subic Bay after mine-clearance
operations off North Vietnam employing RH-53 helicopters.**

Below: *Guadalcanal* **(LPH-7) in the Atlantic. The helicopters are
CH-46 Sea Knights and CH-53 Sea Stallions.**

▶ The flight deck is marked out with five helo spots along the port side and two to starboard. No catapults or arresting wires are fitted. Helicopter assault operations are directed from a specialised Command Centre housed in the island. The radar outfit is austere: air search and aircraft control antennae are fitted but these ships do not have the large 3-D antennae of the first-line carriers.

As completed, the *Iwo Jima* class had two twin 3-inch (76mm) mountings at the forward end of the island and two further mountings just below the after end of the flight deck. Between 1970 and 1974 the after port mounting and the first of the two forward mountings were replaced by BPDMS launchers.

From 1972 until 1974 *Guam* was test ship for the Sea Control Ship concept. In this role she operated ASW helicopters and a squadron of marine AV-8 Harrier aircraft. A new tactical command centre was installed and carrier-controlled approach (CCA) radar fitted. Although operations with the Harrier were particularly successful and have been continued on a routine basis in the larger Tarawa-class LHAs, the Sea Control Ship did not find favour with the US Navy, and *Guam* has since reverted to her assault ship role.

The Iwo Jima class generally operates in conjunction with ships of the LPD, LSD and LST types. Although *Inchon,* the last ship built, carries two LCVPs, the LPHs have no significant ability to land troops, equipment and supplies by any means other than by helicopter. The troops are therefore lightly equipped and would be employed as an advance echelon, landing behind the enemy's shore defences and relying on a follow-up frontal assault staged by more heavily equipped units brought ashore by landing-craft from the other vessels in the squadron.

Above: A Marine AV-8A Harrier STOVL aircraft on the after aircraft elevator of an assault ship of the Iwo Jima class.

Below: Bow view of *Guam* (LPH-9). A BPDMS launcher is visible immediately forward of the island.

Austin

Completed:	1965-71.
Names:	LPD 4 *Austin;* LPD 5 *Ogden;* LPD 6 *Duluth;* LPD 7 *Cleveland;* LPD 8 *Dubuque;* LPD 9 *Denver;* LPD 10 *Juneau;* LPD 11 *Coronado;* LPD 12 *Shreveport;* LPD 13 *Nashville;* LPD 14 *Trenton;* LPD 15 *Ponce.*
Displacement:	10,000t light; 16,900t full load.
Dimensions:	570 oa x 84 x 23ft (173.3 x 25.6 x 7m).
Propulsion:	2-shaft geared steam turbines; 24,000shp = 20kts.
Armament:	4 3-inch (76mm) Mk 33 (2x2).
Aircraft:	up to 6 CH-46D (see notes).
Troops:	840-930.
Landing-craft:	1 LCU, 3 LCM-6.
Sensors:	*Surveillance:* SPS-40, SPS-10.

The Austin class is a development of the Raleigh class, which instituted the LPD concept. The major modification was the insertion of a 50ft (15.2m) hull section forward of the docking-well. This resulted in a significant increase in vehicle space and cargo capacity (3,900 tons compared to only 2,000 tons for the Raleigh class). The additional length available for flying operations enabled a large telescopic hangar to be worked in immediately aft of the superstructure, giving these ships the maintenance facilities which were lacking in the Raleigh class. The main body of the hangar is 58-64ft (17.7-19.5m) in length and 19-24ft (5.8-7.3m) in width; the telescopic extension increases overall length to 80ft (24.4m).

Troop accommodation and docking-well capacity are identical to those of *Raleigh,* except that LPD 7-13 are configured as amphibious squadron (PhibRon) flagships and can accommodate only 840 troops. The latter ships can be outwardly distinguished by their extra bridge level.

Two of the original four twin 3-inch (76mm) mountings, together with all fire-control radars, were removed in the late 1970s. The class is scheduled to receive two Phalanx CIWS guns as soon as these become available.

In October 1980 *Coronado* was temporarily redesignated AGF as a replacement for the Command Ship *La Salle* (see Raleigh class), which is at present undergoing refit.

Below: *Coronado* (LPD-11) operating in company with an assault ship of the Iwo Jima class as part of an Amphibious Squadron.

Bottom: *Juneau* (LPD-10) with CH-46 Sea Knight and CH-53 Sea Stallion assault helicopters on her flight deck.

Raleigh

Completed: 1962-63.
Names: LPD 1 *Raleigh;* LPD 2 *Vancouver.*
Displacement: 8,040t light; 13,900t full load.
Dimensions: 522 oa x 84 x 21ft (158.4 x 25.6 x 6.4m).
Propulsion: 2-shaft geared steam turbines; 24,000shp = 20kts.
Armament: 6 3-inch (76mm) Mk 33 (3x2).
Troops: 930.
Landing-craft: 1 LCU, 3 LCM-6.
Sensors: *Surveillance:* SPS-40, SPS-10.

Raleigh was the prototype of a new amphibious class employing the "balanced load" concept. Previous amphibious task forces carried troops in Attack Transports (APA), cargo in Attack Cargo Ships (AKA), and landing-craft and tanks in Dock Landing Ships (LSD). The basic principle of the "balanced force" concept is that these three capabilities are combined in a single hull. The docking-well in the Raleigh class therefore occupies only the after part of the ship, while forward of the well there are vehicle decks, cargo

holds and substantial troop accommodation decks. The well itself measures 168ft x 50ft (51.2 x 15.2m) – less than half the length of the docking-well in the most modern LSDs – and is served overhead by six monorail cars, which load cargo into the awaiting landing-craft. The docking-well can accommodate one LCU and three LCM-6s, or four LCM-8s. Two further LCM-6s and four LCPLs are carried at the after end of the superstructure, and are handled by a large crane.

The docking-well is covered by a helicopter landing platform, which can receive any of the major types of helicopter in service with the Marines. The Raleigh class, unlike the later Austins, has no hangar or maintenance facilities and therefore relies on an accompanying LPH or LHA to provide helicopters for vertical assault operations. The flight deck can also be used as additional vehicle space, and there are ramps connecting the flight deck, the vehicle decks and the docking-well.

A third ship of the class, *La Salle*, serves as a Command Ship for the US Middle East Force. She was specially converted for this role and is now numbered AGF 3.

Below: *Vancouver* (LPD-2), with marines on her flight deck. No hangar or maintenance facilities for helicopters are provided.

LSD 41

Completed: 1984 onwards.
Name: LSD 41 *Whidbey Island* (building).
Displacement: 11,140t light; 15,745t full load.
Dimensions: 609 oa x 84 x 20ft (185.6 x 25.6 x 5.9m).
Propulsion: 2-shaft diesels; 4 SEMT-Pielstick 16-cyl., 34,000shp = 20kts.
Armament: 2 Phalanx CIWS.
Troops: 340.
Landing-craft: 4 LCAC.
Sensors: *Surveillance:* SPS-55.

The LSD 41 design was prepared in the mid-1970s as a replacement for the eight Thomaston-class ships. The project was subjected to delaying tactics by the Carter Administration pending a reassessment of the Navy's requirement for amphibious lift. In 1981, however, pressure from Congress compelled the Administration to order the prototype for the class, and nine follow-on ships are included in the first 5-year programme of the Reagan Administration.

Although not a particularly innovative design, the LSD 41 shows a number of improvements over its immediate predecessor, the Anchorage class. The

large flight deck aft extends right to the stern, and is strong enough to accept the powerful CH-53E Super Stallion cargo-carrying helicopter now entering service with the Marines. The docking-well is identical in width to that of earlier LSDs but is 10ft (3m) longer than that of *Anchorage*. It is designed to accommodate four of the new air-cushion landing-craft (LCAC), with which it is intended to replace all conventional LCU-type landing-craft in the late 1980s. The two experimental craft at present being evaluated, the Jeff-A and Jeff-B AALCs, are 90ft (30.2m) and 87ft (26.4m) long respectively, and 47-8ft (14.3-14.6m) wide. Both have bow and stern ramps and can carry a single M-60 tank, with an alternative loading of six towed howitzers and trucks or 120,000lb (54,545kg) of cargo. This is a lower lift capacity than the conventional LCU, but the LCAC will compensate for this by carrying its load to the beach at a speed of 50 knots.

The LSD 41 will be built by modular construction techniques, and differs from previous amphibious vessels in adopting diesel propulsion in place of steam turbines. Four SEMT-Pielstick diesels, manufactured under licence, will be installed in two independent paired units. An annual fuel saving of 20 million gallons over a steam plant of similar power is anticipated.

Below: Artist's impression showing how the new dock landing ships will be able to operate four air cushion landing craft, each capable of lifting an M60 tank or 120,000lb of cargo.

Anchorage

Completed:	1969-72.
Names:	LSD 36 *Anchorage;* LSD 37 Portland; LSD 38 *Pensacola;* LSD 39 *Mount Vernon;* LSD 40 *Fort Fisher.*
Displacement:	8,600t light; 13,700t full load.
Dimensions:	553 oa × 84 × 19ft (168.6 × 25.6 × 5.6m).
Propulsion:	2-shaft geared steam turbines; 24,000shp = 20kts.
Armament:	6 3-inch (76mm) Mk 33 (3×2).
Troops:	375
Landing-craft:	3 LCU, 1 LCM-6.
Sensors:	*Surveillance:* SPS-40, SPS-10.

The five dock landing ships of the Anchorage class were among the last units to be completed in the large amphibious ship programme of the 1960s. In spite of the advent of the LPD with its "balanced load" concept, there was still a requirement for LSDs to carry additional landing-craft to the assault area. The Anchorage class was therefore built to replace the ageing war-built vessels, which had inadequate speed for the new PhibRons. It is a

development of the Thomaston class, from which its ships can be distinguished by their tripod mast and their longer hull.

The docking-well measures 430ft by 50ft (131 x 15.2m)—an increase of 30ft (9m) in length over the Thomastons—and can accommodate three of the big LCUs or nine LCM-8s, with an alternative loading of 50 LVTP-7s. There is space on deck for a single LCM-6, and an LCPL and an LCVP are carried on davits. As in the Thomaston class, there are vehicle decks above the docking-well amidships, served by two 50-ton cranes. The Anchorage class was designed to transport up to 30 helicopters, and there is a removable flight deck aft for heavy-lift cargo helicopters.

The sensor outfit and armament are on a par with the contemporary LPDs of the Austin class (which are described on pages 114-115). Four twin 3-inch (76mm) mountings were originally fitted, but one was removed, together with all fire control radars, in the late 1970s. The mountings forward of the bridge are enclosed in GRP shields. Two Phalanx CIWS guns will be fitted when the mounting becomes available.

Below: _Pensacola_ (LSD-38) with an LCU entering the large docking well. The flight deck is a temporary structure, and can be easily removed if required.

Thomaston

Completed:	1954-7.
Names:	LSD 28 *Thomaston;* LSD 29 *Plymouth Rock;* LSD 30 *Fort Snelling;* LSD 31 *Point Defiance;* LSD 32 *Spiegel Grove;* LSD 33 *Alamo;* LSD 34 *Hermitage;* LSD 35 *Monticello.*
Displacement:	6,880t light; 11,270-12,150t full load.
Dimensions:	510 oa x 84 x 19ft (155.5 x 25.6 x 5.8m).
Propulsion:	2-shaft geared steam turbines; 24,000shp = 22.5kts.
Armament:	6 3-inch (76mm) Mk 33 (3x2).
Troops:	340.
Landing-craft	3 LCU.
Sensors:	*Surveillance:* SPS-6, SPS-10.

The Thomaston class was the first postwar LSD design and was a result of the renewed interest in amphibious operations during the Korean War. The basic conception of the wartime LSD was retained but the Thomaston class incorporated a number of improvements. The ships have a large, more seaworthy hull, with greater sheer and flare in the bows, and can steam at a sustained speed of over 20 knots compared to only 15 knots for their war-built counterparts. The docking-well, which measures 391ft by 48ft (119.1 x 14.6m), is wider and more than half as long again, and can accommodate three LCUs or nine LCM-8s. There is a vehicle deck amidships but no access to the docking-well. Cargo and vehicles are therefore preloaded in the landing-craft or handled by the two 50-ton cranes. The after part of the docking-well is covered by a short removable platform for cargo-carrying helicopters, but there are no hangar or maintenance facilities.

As completed, the Thomaston class were armed with eight twin 3-inch (76mm) mountings but five of these, together with all fire-control radars, have since been removed.

In 1980 *Spiegel Grove* conducted evaluation trials for the Jeff-B aircushion landing-craft (AALC). Three such craft could be accommodated in the docking-well of the Thomaston class, but it is possible that some of these ships will be retired before the production LCAC enters service.

Above: An LCU is about to enter the docking well of an LSD of the Thomaston class. Three LCUs can operate from the well.

Left: The dock landing ship *Hermitage* (LSD-34). These ships will shortly be replaced by the new LSD-41 class.

Newport

Completed:	1969-72.
Names:	LST 1179 *Newport;* LST 1180 *Maniwotoc;* LST 1181 *Sumter;* LST 1182 *Fresno;* LST 1183 *Peoria;* LST 1184 *Frederick;* LST 1185 *Schenectady;* LST 1186 *Cayuga;* LST 1187 *Tuscaloosa;* LST 1188 *Saginaw;* LST 1189 *San Bernadino;* LST 1190 *Boulder;* LST 1191 *Racine;* LST 1192 *Spartanburg County;* LST 1193 *Fairfax County;* LST 1194 *La Moure County;* LST 1195 *Barbour County;* LST 1196 *Harlan County;* LST 1197 *Barnstable County;* LST 1198 *Bristol County.*
Displacement:	8,342t full load.
Dimensions:	562 oa x 70 x 18ft (171.3 x 21.2 x 5.3m).
Propulsion:	2-shaft diesels; 6 GM (1179-81)/Alco (others); 16,500bhp = 20kts.
Armament:	4 3-inch (76mm) Mk 33 (2x2).
Sensors:	*Surveillance:* SPS-10.

The twenty LSTs of the Newport class are larger and faster than the war-built vessels they replaced. In order to match the 20-knot speed of the other amphibious units built during the 1960s the traditional bow doors were suppressed in favour of a 112ft (34m) ramp which is lowered over the bows of the ship between twin fixed derrick arms. This arrangement also allowed for an increase in draught in line with the increase in displacement.

Right: Amphibious personnel carriers (LVTP-7) return to the tank landing ship *Newport* (LST-1179) during an Atlantic exercise.

Below: A tank landing ship of the Newport class unloads vehicles via a bow ramp slung between its massive "jaws".

There is a large integral flight deck aft for utility helicopters. Pontoons can be slung on either side of the flight deck for use in landing operations. Each can carry an MBT and they can be mated with the stern gate. They are handled by twin derricks located immediately aft of the staggered funnel uptakes.

Below decks there is a total parking area of 19,000sq ft (5,300m^2) for a cargo capacity of 500 tons of vehicles. The forecastle is connected to the vehicle deck by a ramp and to the flight deck by a passageway through the superstructure. A through-hull bow thruster is provided to maintain the ship's position while unloading offshore.

The twin 3-inch (76mm) gun mounts, located at the after end of the superstructure will be replaced by Phalanx CIWS guns when these become available.

In 1980 *Boulder* and *Racine* were assigned to the Naval Reserve Force.

Support Ships

Yellowstone/Samuel Gompers

Completed: 1967 onwards.
Names: AD 37 *Samuel Gompers;* AD 38 *Puget Sound;*
     AD 41 *Yellowstone;* AD 42 *Acadia;* AD 43 *Cape Cod;*
     AD 44 *Shenandoah* (building).
Displacement: (AD 37,38) 22,200t full load.
     (AD 41-44) 22,800t full load.
Dimensions: 643 oa x 85 x 23ft (196 x 25.9 x 6.9m).
Propulsion: 1-shaft geared steam turbines; 20,000shp = 18kts.
Armament: 4 20mm (4x1) in AD 37-8; 2 40mm (2x1), 2 20mm (2x1)
     in AD 41-4.
Sensors: *Surveillance:* SPS-10.

Samuel Gompers and *Puget Sound* were the Navy's first destroyer tenders
built to a postwar design. They are similar in size and general configuration to
the contemporary SSBN tenders of the Simon Lake class, but were
specifically fitted out to support surface combatants on forward deployment.
They can furnish in-port service to six cruiser/destroyer types alongside
simultaneously. The high-sided hull and the superstructures contain
approximately 60 workshops to enable these ships to maintain and repair
the latest equipment, including missile systems, ASW weapons, advanced

Forward basing for a significant proportion of the US Fleet brings with it a requirement for large numbers of depot ships. Depot ship support is necessarily specialist. Not only are ships designed to support a particular type— eg destroyers, SSBNs, SSNs—but they are frequently equipped to provide spares and repair facilities for a particular class. A large replacement programme has been underway since the mid-1960s and most support ships are modern and well-equipped.

communications and electronics and nuclear propulsion plants. There are two 30-ton kingpost cranes to handle heavier items such as propellers and machinery, and two 6-ton travelling cranes for smaller items of equipment. A hangar and platform were provided for DASH, but the hangar proved too small for manned helicopters and that on *Samuel Gompers* has been converted into a boat repair shop. A single 5-inch/38 cal. gun initially fitted forward of the bridge has now been removed. Plans to fit NATO Sea Sparrow in its place have now been abandoned.

The Yellowstone class is a follow-on design and will replace the ageing tenders of the Dixie class. Improvements over the Gompers class include increased supply and stowage capacity, the fitting of heavier travelling cranes (6.5-ton), the provision of two 50ft (15m) LCM workboats primarily designed for handling weapons, and a rationalised layout of workshops. There is also topside stowage at 01 deck level for spare gas turbines for the DD 963, FFG 7 and PHM 1 types.

Both classes have the Navy Automated Communications System and can accommodate the Commander and staff of a Cruiser-Destroyer Group or a Destroyer Squadron. Two Phalanx CIWS guns will be fitted.

Below: The destroyer tender *Samuel Gompers* (AD-37) can support up to six cruiser/destroyer types alongside simultaneously. The kingpost cranes can handle heavy items such as propellers and machinery, while the two small travelling cranes are used for delivering spares and weapons aboard.

Emory S. Land/L.Y. Spear

Completed: 1970-81.
Names: AS 36 *L.Y. Spear;* AS 37 *Dixon;* AS 39 *Emory S. Land;*
AS 40 *Frank Cable;* AS 41 *McKee.*
Displacement: (AS 36, 37) 12,700t light; 22,628t full load.
(AS 39-41) 13,842t light; 23,000t full load.
Dimensions: 646 oa x 85 x 25ft (196.8 x 25.9 x 7.5m).
Propulsion: 1-shaft geared steam turbines; 20,000shp = 18kts.
Armament: 4 20mm (4x1) in AS 36,7, 2 40mm (2x1), 4 20mm(4x1) in
AS 39-41.
Sensors: *Surveillance:* SPS-10.

Derived from the SSBN tenders of the Simon Lake class, *L.Y. Spear* and
Dixon were the first submarine tenders to be designed to support SSNs, for
which they provide repairs, spare parts, provisions, ordnance and medical
facilities. There are three Ship Alongside Service (SAS) stations supplied
through four switchboards. Services supplied include compressed air,

oxygen, nitrogen, 150-lb (68kg) steam, oil, water and electrical power. A single 15-ton kingpost crane immediately forward of the funnel handles propellers and heavy machinery, and other items of equipment are handled by two 5-ton travelling cranes with a 55ft (17m) outreach, running on tracks which cover the entire midships section. There is a helicopter deck but no hangar or maintenance facilities. Single 5-inch/38 cal. guns initially fitted fore and aft have been removed in favour of a minimal armament of 20mm guns.

The Emory S. Land class is a follow-on design fitted specifically for the support of SSNs of the Los Angeles class. The first two ships are already operational in the Atlantic, and the third will serve in the Pacific. Improvements over the Spear class include an increase in crane capacity—that of the kingpost crane has been doubled in order to handle the heavier machinery of the Los Angles class—and an increase in generating power. There are 53 workshops and 16 magazines on 13 deck levels. Up to four submarines can be supported alongside simultaneously.

Below: The submarine tender *Dixon* (AS-37) at the San Diego Submarine Support Facility. Two SSNs are moored alongside.

Simon Lake

Completed: 1964-5.
Names: AS 33 *Simon Lake;* AS 34 *Canopus.*
Displacement: 21,500t full load.
Dimensions: 644 oa x 85 x 25ft (196.2 x 25.9 x 7.5m).
Propulsion: 1-shaft geared steam turbines; 20,000shp = 18kts.
Armament: 4 3-inch (76mm) Mk 33 (2x2).
Sensors: *Surveillance:* SPS-10.

The two SSBN tenders of the Simon Lake class are larger than their immediate predecessors of the Hunley class and have a much improved layout. The funnel and machinery are well aft, leaving the midships section clear for cranage and services to support up to three submarines lying alongside. There is a full reactor support capability and facilities are provided for the handling, replacement and limited servicing of SLBMs. Both ships were modified 1969-71 to enable them to handle Poseidon, and Simon Lake has recently been fitted for Trident. Two kingpost cranes are located amidships, and there are four smaller cranes. A helicopter platform is provided for VERTREP operations.

A third ship was to have been built under FY 1965, for a total of six SSBN tenders (including the older conversion *Proteus*) to support five SSBN squadrons, but she was not built and only four SSBN squadrons were formed.

Right: The submarine tender *Simon Lake* (AS-33) operating off Hawaii. She and her sister *Canopus* (AS-34) now serve in the Atlantic, where they support the SSBNs of the Lafayette class. The two kingpost cranes can handle the large Poseidon ballistic missiles, and *Simon Lake* has recently been refitted to enable her to handle Trident.

Hunley

Completed: 1961-3.
Names: AS 31 *Hunley;* AS 32 *Holland.*
Displacement: 10,500t standard; 18,300t full load.
Dimensions: 599 oa x 83 x 24ft (182.6 x 25.3 x 7.3m).
Propulsion: 1-shaft diesel-electric; 6 Fairbanks-Morse diesels; 15,000bhp = 19kts.
Armament: 4 20mm (2x2).
Sensors: *Surveillance:* SPS-10.

These were the first purpose-built SSBN tenders. They can supply services to three submarines alongside simultaneously and support a squadron of nine. There are 52 workshops and extensive stowage facilities, including vertical stowage for SLBMs. These were originally handled by a massive 32-ton hammerhead crane with athwartships travel, but this has since been replaced by two conventional kingpost cranes. There is a helicopter platform aft for VERTREP operations. Both ships were modified 1973-5 to enable them to handle Poseidon.

Right: *Hunley* (AS31), the first purpose-built tender for the navy's Polaris submarines. Here the original distinctive hammerhead crane has been replaced by two conventional kingpost cranes. The helicopter pad aft allows for VERTREP operations, facilitating the transfer of spares.

Replenishment Ships

Kilauea

Completed: 1968-72.
Names: T-AE 26 *Kilauea;* AE 27 *Butte;* AE 28 *Santa Barbara;*
AE 29 *Mount Hood;* AE 33 *Shasta;*
AE 34 *Mount Baker;* AE 35 *Kiska.*
Displacement: 20,500t full load.
Dimensions: 564 oa x 81 x 26ft (171.9 x 24.7 x 7.8m).
Propulsion: 1-shaft geared steam turbine; 22,000shp = 20kts.
Armament: 4 3-inch (76mm) Mk 33 (2x2)—not in T-AE 26.
Helicopters: 2 UH-46 Sea Knight.
Sensors: *Surveillance:* SPS-10.

The eight ammunition ships of the Kilauea class belong to the generation of underway replenishment vessels constructed during the 1960s. They are similar in size to the combat stores ships of the Mars class, but specialise in the

No other navy in the world can approach the underway replenishment capability of the US Fleet. The requirement for regular distant deployments far from the United States has brought with it the need for vast numbers of specialist auxiliary vessels to supply the fleet with oil, munitions and combat stores. Until recently these ships were manned by naval personnel, but a shortage of enlisted men has led to the transfer of a number of vessels to the civilian-manned Military Sealift Command (MSC).

transfer of missiles and other munitions. Improvements in layout include the merging of the bridge and hangar structures into a single block, leaving the entire forward and midships areas clear for transfer operations. The central section of the hull is a deck higher than that of the Mars class, providing the additional internal volume necessary for the stowage of missiles. Cargo capacity is approximately 6,500 tons. Four transfer stations are provided on either side forward of the bridge, and there is a further pair abreast the funnel and another at the after end of the hangar. The second and sixth pairs of transfer stations are fitted with booms in addition to the customary constant-tension gear. Fin stabilisers ensure a steady platform for the safe transfer of the ships' delicate cargo.

The twin hangars are 50ft long and 16-18ft (15.2 x 4.7-5.3m) wide and can accommodate two UH-46 VERTREP helicopters. All ships initially had two twin 3-inch (76mm) mounts and Mk 56 GFCS on the hangar roof but these were removed in the late 1970s. A plan to install NATO Sea Sparrow was abandoned, but two Phalanx CIWS guns will eventually be fitted.

Below: The ammunition ship *Kilauea* (AE-26) underway.

Suribachi

Completed: 1956-9.
Names: AE 21 *Suribachi;* AE 22 *Mauna Kea;* AE 23 *Nitro;*
AE 24 *Pyro;* AE 25 *Haleakala.*
Displacement: 10,000t standard; 17,500t full load.
Dimensions: 512 oa x 72 x 29ft (156.1 x 21.9 x 8.8m).
Propulsion: 1-shaft geared steam turbine; 16,000shp = 20.6kts.
Armament: 4 3-inch (76mm) Mk 33 (2x2).
Sensors: SPS-10.

Built from the keel up as Navy ships, the Suribachi class were among the first specialised underway replenishment vessels built postwar. As completed, they were equipped with conventional mercantile kingposts and booms for the transfer of bombs and other munitions. Elevators were provided for the internal handling of ammunition and explosives, and the design incorporated air conditioning and the latest methods of stowage. A sixth ship was to have been built under the FY 1959 Programme but was cancelled.

Soon after completion, all five ships underwent an extensive modernisation to enable them to handle the new surface-to-air missiles. Three holds were rigged for the stowage of missiles up to the size of Talos, and fully mechanised handling facilities were provided to move the missiles to the transfer stations. The Fast Automatic Shuttle Transfer (FAST) system pioneered by the combat stores ships of the Mars class was installed, resulting in safer missile handling and reduced transfer times. The Suribachi class now has three kingposts, the first and third of which have constant-tension transfer stations on either side.

As completed, these ships had two superfiring twin 3-inch mountings on the forecastle and a similar arrangement aft. Mk 56 and Mk 63 GFCS were provided. When the ships underwent modernisation in the mid-1960s, the after mountings and the fire-control systems were removed and a large flight deck for VERTREP helicopters was fitted above the stern. In some units the forward guns have been relocated side by side and given GRP gunshields. *Mauna Kea* and *Pyro* have recently been placed in reserve.

Below: The ammunition ship *Suribachi* (AE-21) one of the first underway replenishment vessels built postwar for the US Navy.

Bottom: *Suribachi* and her sisters were extensively modernised during the 1960s. Note the large helicopter platform aft.

Mars

Completed:	1963-70.
Names:	AFS 1 *Mars;* AFS 2 *Sylvania;* AFS 3 *Niagara Falls;* AFS 4 *White Plains;* AFS 5 *Concord;* AFS 6 *San Diego;* AFS 7 *San Jose.*
Displacement:	16,500t full load.
Dimensions:	581 oa x 79 x 24ft (177.1 x 24.1 x 7.3m).
Propulsion:	1-shaft geared steam turbine; 22,000shp = 20kts.
Armament:	4 3-inch (76mm) Mk 33 (2x2).
Helicopters:	2 UH-46 Sea Knight.
Sensors:	*Surveillance:* SPS-10.

The seven combat stores ships of the Mars class were the first of a new generation of under-way replenishment vessels completed during the 1960s to support carrier task force deployments. They combine the functions of store ships (AF), stores-issue ships (AKS), and aviation store ships (AVS). Unlike the contemporary AOEs of the Sacramento class, however, they carry no fuel oil or other liquid cargo.

They were the first ships to incorporate the Fast Automatic Shuttle Transfer system (FAST), which revolutionised the handling of stores and munitions. Five "M" frames replace the conventional kingposts and booms of previous vessels and these have automatic tensioning devices to keep the transfer lines taut while replenishing. Cargo capacity is 7,000 tons in five cargo holds. Computers provide up-to-the-minute data on stock status, with the data displayed on closed-circuit television (CCTV). The propulsion system is also fully automated and can be controlled from the bridge to ensure quick response during transfer operations. The ships normally steam on only two boilers, with the third shut down for maintenance.

Twin helicopter hangars, 47-51ft long and 16-23ft wide (143-15.5 x 4.9-7m) are provided for VERTREP helicopters, enabling the ships to undertake vertical replenishment operations within a task force spread over a wide area.

As completed, the Mars class had four twin 3-inch mounts and the Mk 56 GFCS. Two of the twin mounts and the fire-control system were removed in the late 1970s.

Below: The combat stores ship *Mars* (AFS-1) underway off Hawaii. They were the first US ships to have the FAST transfer system.

AO
Cimarron

Completed: 1980 onwards.
Names: AO 177 *Cimarron;* AO 178 *Monongahela;*
AO 179 *Merrimack;* AO 180 *Willamette;* T-AO 186 *Platte.*
Displacement: 27,500t full load.
Dimensions: 592 oa x 88 x 34ft (178 x 26 8 x 10.2m).
Propulsion: 1-shaft geared steam turbine; 24,000shp = 20kts.
Armament: 2 Phalanx CIWS (not in T-AO 186).

The new fleet oilers of the Cimarron class are the first ships in that category to be completed since the mid-1950s. Large numbers are planned as replacements for the war-built oilers of the Mispillion and Ashtaboula classes, which, although extensively modernised in the 1960s, are now

more than 35 years old. The US Navy has a requirement for 21 fleet oilers, and this figure can only be achieved by new construction on a massive scale.

The Cimarron-class oilers are significantly smaller than previous vessels. They have been deliberately "sized" to provide two complete refuellings of a fossil-fuelled carrier and six to eight escorts, and have a total capacity of 120,000 barrels of fuel oil. There are four replenishment stations to port and three to starboard, and there is a large platform aft for VERTREP helicopters, but no hangar or support facilities are provided.

These ships have a distinctive elliptical underwater bow for improved seakeeping. Unlike previous AOs, they have a single superstructure block aft incorporating the bridge. Originally it was envisaged that they would have a crew of only 135, but this was increased to 181 in order to provide sufficient personnel to carry out maintenance on prolonged deployments. Later ships of the class will be manned by the Military Sealift Command (MSC) – these units will not be fitted with the Phalanx CIWS gun.

Left: The oiler *Cimarron* (AO-177) on sea trials in the Gulf of Mexico following her completion in 1980.

Below: *Cimarron* is smaller than previous US Navy oilers. Note the block bridge structure and the helicopter landing pad aft.

Bottom: The rig is biased towards replenishment operations on the port side to facilitate the refuelling of carriers.

AO
Neosho

Completed: 1954-56.
Names: T-AO 143 *Neosho;* T-AO 144 *Mississinewa;*
T-AO 145 *Hassayampa;* T-AO 146 *Kawishiwi;*
T-AO 147 *Truckee;* T-AO 148 *Ponchatoula.*
Displacement: 11,600t light; 38-40,000t full load.
Dimensions: 655 oa x 86 x 35ft (199.6 x 26.2 x 10.7m).
Propulsion: 2-shaft geared steam turbines; 28,000shp = 20kts.
Armament: removed.
Sensors: *Surveillance:* SPS-10.

These were the first major under-way replenishment vessels to be built postwar, and they are the largest fleet oilers in the US Navy. They have a capacity of approximately 180,000 barrels of fuel oil, and have been fitted since the 1960s with a modern rig for abeam replenishment. There is a separate bridge structure with a single pole mast and twin booms forward,

and there are three kingposts and a second pole mast between the bridge and the after structure. The ships of the Neosho class were designed to serve as flagships of the service forces, and were given accommodation for the Service Force Commander and his staff.

As completed, they carried a powerful defensive battery of anti-aircraft guns, comprising single 5-inch (127mm) fore and aft, two twin 3-inch (76mm) mounts on the forecastle and four twin mounts at the corners of the after superstructure. The 5-inch guns were removed in 1960 and three ships – *Neosho, Mississinewa* and *Truckee* – had helicopter platforms fitted above the stern. The number of 3-inch weapons was steadily reduced and they were removed altogether when the ships were transferred to the Military Sealift Comand (MSC) from 1976 onwards. The change in status has not affected their operational deployment in support of the carrier battle groups and amphibious squadrons, but they are now manned by civilians, not regular Navy personnel.

Below: The oiler *Neosho* (AO-143) underway. These ships were the first major underway replenishment vessels built postwar.

Mispillion/Ashtaboula

Completed:	1943-6.
Names:	T-AO 105 *Mispillion;* T-AO 106 *Navasota;*
	T-AO 107 *Passumpsic;* T-AO 108 *Pawcatuck;*
	T-AO 109 *Waccamaw;* AO 51 *Ashtaboula;*
	AO 98 *Caloosahatchee;* AO 99 *Canisteo.*
Displacement:	34,750t full load.
Dimensions:	646/644 oa x 75 x 36/32ft (196.9/196.3 x 22.9 x
	10.8/9.6m).
Propulsion:	2-shaft geared steam turbines; 13,500shp = 16-18kts.
Armament:	2 3-inch (76mm) Mk 26 (2x1) in AO only.
Sensors:	*Surveillance:* SPS-10.

These ships were originally of the war-built Maritime Administration
T3–S2–A1 type but were extensively modernised during the mid-1960s.
Modernisation included a concept known as "jumboisation" in which a 91-
3ft (28m) midships section was inserted, increasing cargo capacity by 50
per cent. A completely new transfer rig was installed. The five ships of the
Mispillion class have four fuelling stations to port and two to starboard.

There is a kingpost aft with constant-tension stations for the transfer of dry stores, and a large flight deck is marked out forward for the operation of VERTREP helicopters. Cargo capacity is 150,000 barrels of fuel oil.

The three ships of the Ashtaboula class underwent a different modification. The rig amidships is similar to that of the Mispillion class except that there is a third fuelling station to starboard. Forward, however, the helicopter landing area has been replaced by a second kingpost with constant-tension transfer stations, and there is a limited capacity for "dry" cargo. Besides fuel oil – 143,000 barrels – they can carry 175 tons of munitions, 250 tons of dry stores and 100 tons of refrigerated stores.

The original armament comprised 5-inch (127mm), 3-inch (76mm) and 40mm guns but these have since been progressively removed. The five ships of the Mispillion class, which were transferred to MSC in 1974-5, are now unarmed. The Ashtaboula class, which is still Navy-manned, has only two single 3-inch guns remaining.

Although virtually rebuilt in the 1960s, these ships are now over 35 years old and they are slow by modern standards. They will have to be replaced in the near future.

Below: The oiler *Ashtaboula* (A0-51) with the Ro-Ro cargo ship *Mercury* (TAKR-10) at Subic Bay in the Philippines.

Sacramento

Completed:	1964-70.
Names:	AOE 1 *Sacramento;* AOE 2 *Camden;* AOE 3 *Seattle;* AOE 4 *Detroit.*
Displacement:	19,200t light; 53,600t full load.
Dimensions:	793 oa x 107 x 39ft (241.7 x 32.6 x 12m).
Propulsion:	2-shaft geared steam turbines; 100,000shp = 26kts.
Armament:	1 NATO Sea Sparrow launcher Mk 29 (1x8); 4 3-inch (76mm). Mk 33 (2x2).
Helicopters:	2 UH-46 Sea Knight.
Sensors:	*Surveillance:* SPS-40, SPS-10. *Fire Control:* 2 Mk 91.

The world's largest under-way replenishment vessels, the fast combat support ships of the Sacramento class are designed to supply a carrier battle group with all its basic needs. They combine the functions of fleet oilers (AO), ammunition ships (AE), stores ships (AF) and cargo ships (AK). They have exceptionally high speed for their type to enable them to keep pace with fleet units. The machinery installed in *Sacramento* and *Camden* is from the cancelled battleship *Kentucky* (BB 66).

Cargo capacity is 177,000 barrels of fuel oil, 2,150 tons of munitions, 250 tons of dry stores and 250 tons of refrigerated stores. The Sacramento

class was one of the first two designs to employ the FAST automatic transfer system. There are four refuelling stations to port and two to starboard—an arrangement which reflects their primary mission in support of the carriers—and there are three constant-tension transfer stations for dry stores to port and four to starboard. Aft there is a large helicopter deck with a three-bay hangar for VERTREP helicopters; each hangar bay is 47-52ft long and 17-19ft wide (14.3-15.8 x 5.2-5.8m).

As completed, these ships each had four twin 3-inch (76mm) mounts, together with Mk 56 GFCS. The forward pair of mountings and the fire-control systems were removed in the mid-1970s and have now been replaced by a NATO Sea Sparrow launcher with twin Mk 91 fire-control systems side by side atop the bridge. Two Phalanx CIWS guns are to be fitted.

The Sacramento class proved very expensive, and a fifth ship planned for FY 1968 was not built. Instead the smaller and less costly Wichita-class AOR was developed as an alternative. The requirement for a twelfth AOE/AOR-type vessel to support the twelfth carrier battle group remains, however. A fifth AOE was again planned for the FY 1980 Programme, and, although this ship did not materialise, the first of a new series is scheduled for FY 1984.

Below: The first combat support ship *Camden* **(AOE-2). These ships were built to accompany the US Navy's carrier battle groups. They proved very costly and were succeeded by the slower AOR type.**

AOR

Wichita

Completed: 1969-75.
Names: AOR 1 *Wichita;* AOR 2 *Milwaukee;* AOR 3 *Kansas City;*
AOR 4 *Savannah;* AOR 5 *Wabash;* AOR 6 *Kalamazoo;*
AOR 7 *Roanoke.*
Displacement: 38,100t full load.
Dimensions: 659 oa x 96 x 33ft (206.9 x 29.3 x 10.2m).
Propulsion: 2-shaft geared steam turbines; 32,000shp = 20kts.
Armament: 1 NATO Sea Sparrow launcher Mk 29 (1x8) in AOR 3,7;
4 3-inch (76mm) Mk 33 (2x2) in AOR 1, 4, 6;
2/4 20mm (2/4x1) in AOR 2,7.
Helicopters: 2 UH-46 Sea Knights in AOR 2-3,5,7.
Sensors: *Surveillance:* SPS-10.
Fire Control: 2 Mk 91 in AOR 3,7.

The Wichita-class replenishment oilers, like the fast combat support ships of
the Sacramento class, are designed for the support of the carrier battle
groups. They are smaller vessels with much-reduced speed but have proved
to be very successful ships. They carry a similar quantity of fuel oil to the
larger AOEs but have only a limited capacity for provisions and munitions.
This is reflected in their rig; there are four fuelling stations to port and three
to starboard, but only two positions on either beam for the transfer of dry
stores. Cargo capacity is 160,000 barrels of fuel, 600 tons of munitions,
200 tons of dry stores and 100 tons of refrigerated stores.

AOR 1-6 were completed with two twin 3-inch (76mm) mountings above
the flight deck aft, together with the Mk 56 GFCS. The last ship, however,
was completed with a double helicopter hangar built around the funnel, and

all other ships are now being similarly fitted. The hangars are 62-3ft long and 19-21ft wide (18-19.2 x 5.8-6.4m). The guns are being replaced by a NATO Sea Sparrow launcher at the after end of the hangar, with a pair of Mk 91 fire control radars atop twin lattice masts forward of the funnel. An interim armament of 20mm guns has been fitted in some ships without 3-inch guns. All will eventually receive two Phalanx CIWS guns.

The Wichita class normally operates on only two boilers while maintenance is carried out on the third. The ships of the class can sustain 18 knots while operating in this mode.

Below: The replenishment oiler *Wichita* (AOR-1). Although slower than the AOEs these have proved to be very successful ships.

Bottom: *Wichita* underway. The twin 3-inch guns are being replaced by a large double helicopter hangar and missile launchers.

Weapons and Sensors

Carrier-Borne Fixed-Wing Aircraft

F-14A Tomcat

In service: 1972.
Weight: 72,000lb (32,727kg) max.
Dimensions: 62 x 38 (swept) x 16ft (18.9 x 11.6 x 4.9m)
Fleet Air Defence fighter with AWG-9 missile-control system and six Phoenix AAMs. Two 12-plane squadrons in later CVs.

F-4J Phantom

In service: 1966
Weight: 54,600lb (24,818kg) max.
Dimensions: 58 x 38 x 16ft (17.8 x 11.7 x 5m).
All-weather multi-purpose fighter with Sparrow and Sidewinder AAMs. Two 12-plane squadrons in earlier CVs. To be replaced by F/A-18 Hornet in mid-1980s.

Below: The A-6 Intruder has been the standard all-weather attack aircraft aboard US carriers since the mid-1960s.

Most US Navy weapons systems remain in service for a considerable number of years, and after that time are generally replaced by systems which represent a "quantum jump" in terms of their technology. Existing equipment therefore receives frequent updates to improve performance and reliability. This applies particularly to electronics and avionics, and few US ships emerge from even routine refits without modifications which facilitate the collection, analysis and transfer of action data.

A-7E Corsair

In service: 1969
Weight: 42,000lb (19,090kg) max.
Dimensions: 46 x 39 x 16ft (14.1 x 11:8 x 4.9m).
Light attack aircraft with limited all-weather and night capability, 16,000lb (7,270kg) of ordnance. Two 12-plane squadrons in all CVs. To be replaced by F/A-18 Hornet in mid-1980s.

A-6E Intruder

In service: 1970.
Weight: 60,400lb (27,455kg) max.
Dimensions: 55 x 53 x 16ft (16.7 x 16.2 x 4.9m).
All-weather and night attack aircraft. 14,000lb (6,364kg) of ordnance. One 10-plane squadron + 4 KA-6D tankers in all CVs.

Below: Ground crew prepare an A-7 Corsair on the flight deck of *America* **(CV-66). Two squadrons operate from each carrier.**

E-2C Hawkeye
In service: 1973.
Weight: 51,570lb (23,440kg) max.
Dimensions: 58 x 81 x 18ft (17.6 x 24.6 x 5.6m).
Airborne Early Warning (AEW) aircraft. 24ft (7.3m) diameter saucer-shaped radome for APS-125 UHF radar. Four-plane detachment in all CVs.

EA-6B Prowler
In service: 1971.
Weight: 58,500lb (26,590kg) max.
Dimensions: 59 x 53 x 16ft (18.1 x 16.2 x 5m).
ECM variant of Intruder. Four-plane squadron in all CVs.

S-3A Viking
In service: 1974.
Weight: 52,540lb (23,882kg) max.
Dimensions: 53 x 69 x 23ft (16.3 x 20.9 x 6.9m).
ASW aircraft with onboard AYK-30 digital computer for processing sonobuoy data, four Mk 46 torpedoes, and 3,000lb other ordnance. One 10-plane squadron in all CVs except Midway class.

Above right: An E-2C Hawkeye AEW aircraft comes in to land.

Right: The S-3A Viking is a sophisticated ASW aircraft.

Surveillance Radars
SPS-48
In service: 1965 (first operational installation).
Long-range (230nm, 426km) 3-D radar used to provide target data for Terrier/Standard ER missile in CGs and for aircraft control in CVs. Large square planar antenna.

SPS-30
In service: 1962.
Long-range 3-D radar used for aircraft control in older CVs. Large solid dish antenna with prominent feed-horn. Being replaced by SPS-48.

Right: The SPS-48 is the standard 3-D radar on US cruisers.

Below: Air detection and tracking consoles on *Mount Whitney*.

SPS-39/52

In service: 1960/1966.

3-D radar used to provide target data for Tartar/Standard MR missile in DDGs and FFGs. Rectangular planar antenna.

SPS-49

In service: 1976.

Long-range air search radar. In FFG-7 and to be retro-fitted to all major classes in place of SPS-37/37A/43/43A. Elliptical lattice antenna.

SPS-37A/43A

In service: 1961.

Long-range (300nm, 556km) air search radar in CVs. 13-metre (42.6ft) rectangular lattice antenna.

Below: Two frigates of the Brooke (foreground) and Knox classes, displaying typical small-ship radar arrays. The square planar antenna is an SPS-52, while the Knox has the SPS-40 air search antenna. Both ships have the SPS-10 surface radar.

SPS-37/43
In service: 1960/1961.
Long-range (230nm, 426km) air search radar in CGs and some DDs and DDGs. Rectangular mattress antenna.

SPS-40
In service: 1962.
Medium-range (150-80nm, 278-334-km)) air search radar in DDs, FFs, some DDGs, and amphibious vessels. Elliptical lattice antenna with feed-horn above.

SPS-55
In service: 1975.
Surface search radar. Has replaced SPS-10 in new construction.

SPS-10
In service: 1953.
Surface search radar. Standard on all but most recent units. To be upgraded to SPS-67

Surface-to-Air Missiles

Standard SM-1ER (RIM-67A)

In service:	1970.
Length:	27ft (8.23m).
Range:	35nm (65km).
Fire Control:	SPG-55 with Mk 76 MFCS.
Guidance:	Semi-active homing.
Remarks:	Terrier replacement on CGs. Twin launcher. Mk 10 (40-60 missiles—80 in CGN 9).

Standard SM-1MR (RIM-66B)

In service:	1970.
Length:	15ft (4.57m).
Range:	15nm (27.8km).
Fire Control:	SPG-51 with Mk 74 MFCS.
Guidance:	Semi-active homing.
Remarks:	Same missile as above but without booster. Tartar replacement on DDGs, FFGs and new CGNs. Twin launcher Mk 11 (42 missiles), single launcher Mk 13 (40 missiles), single launcher Mk 22 (16 missiles) or twin launcher Mk 26 (24-44 missiles).

NATO Sea Sparrow (RIM-7H)

In service:	1977.
Length:	12ft (3.65m).
Range:	8nm (14.8km).
Fire Control:	Mk 91.
Guidance:	Continuous Wave (CW) semi-active homing.
Remarks:	Improved Point Defense Missile System (IPDMS) in CVs, Spruance-class DDs and large replenishment vessels. High performance version of Sparrow missile with folding fins and specially designed lightweight 8-round box launcher (Mk 29). Manual reloading. Automatic tracking.

Sea Sparrow (RIM-7E)

In service:	1969.
Length:	12ft (3.65m).
Range:	5nm (9.27km).
Fire Control:	Mk 115.
Guidance:	Continuous Wave (CW) semi-active homing.
Remarks:	Basic Point Defense Missile System (BPDMS) in CVs and Knox-class FFs. Fired from modified ASROC launcher (Mk 25) on modified 3-inch (76mm) gun carriage. Mk 115 illuminator manually trained on target.

Above right: A Standard SM-1 medium-range (MR) missile leaves the forward launcher of a cruiser of the California class. The SM-1 has now replaced the Tartar missile on destroyers and frigates fitted with the twin-arm Mk 11 launcher or the single-arm Mk 13 and Mk 22 launchers. It is also fired from the twin-arm Mk 26 or the single Mk 13 launcher aboard latest CGNs.

Right: An RIM-7E Sea Sparrow missile is fired from one of three Mk 25 launchers aboard *Enterprise* (CVN-65). The RIM-7E was adapted from the air-launched Sparrow missile and forms the basis of the US Navy's Basic Point Defense Missile System (BPDMS). It is fired from a modified ASROC launcher and is now being superseded by the RIM-7H version.

ASW Weapons and Sensors

LAMPS (Light Airborne Multi-Purpose System)
In service: 1971.

Manned anti-submarine helicopters used to localise and attack submarine contacts detected by shipboard sonar. Fitted with surface search radar, MAD and sonobuoys. Current LAMPS I is SH-2F Seasprite. Will be replaced by SH-60B Seahawk (LAMPS III) in mid-1980s.

ASROC (RUR-5A)
In service: 1961.
Length: 15ft (4.6m).
Range: 6nm (11.1km).
Payload: Mk 46 homing torpedo or nuclear depth bomb Mk 17.
Fire Control: Mk 114/Mk 116.

Anti-submarine rocket fitted in all major surface units up to FFG 7. Fired from octuple Mk 16 launcher or Mk 10/Mk 26 SAM launchers. Cannot be guided in flight. Will be phased out in late 1980s.

Mk 46 Torpedo
In service: 1967.
Length: 8.5ft (2.6m)
Diameter: 12.75in (324mm).
Guidance: active/passive acoustic homing.

Fired from triple trainable or single fixed Mk 32 tubes on all surface warships. Normal payload of ASROC missile. NEARTIP update.

SQS-26/53
In service: 1962/1975.

Large LF bow sonar. Simultaneous active/passive operation in a variety of modes (incl. bottom bounce, convergence zone). Detection ranges out to first convergence zone (25-35nm, 46.3-65km). Fitted in most FFs and all major surface units since mid-1960s. SQS-53 has solid-state electronics and digital interface with Mk 116 UFCS.

SQS-23
In service: 1958.

Predecessor of above. LF sonar with detection ranges of 6nm (11.1km) approx. In all major surface warships built late 1950s/early 1960s. To be upgraded to SQQ-23 status with active/passive operation.

SQS-56
In service: 1977.

Austere MF hull sonar designed for FFG 7. Latest technology but modest range.

SQS-35
In service: 1968.

Independent MF variable depth sonar fitted in stern counter of Knox-class FFs. SQR-18 passive array (in service 1978) can be streamed from towed body.

Top right: LAMPS helicopters were introduced in the 1970s and are standard on antisubmarine destroyers and frigates.

Centre: An ASROC missile launched from the frigate *Brooke* (FFG-1). ASROC is fitted in all except the latest escorts.

Right: A lightweight Mk 46 antisubmarine torpedo is launched from the standard triple Mk 32 tubes fitted in most US escorts.

Anti-Ship Missiles, and Guns

Tomahawk (BGM-109)

In service: 1983 (scheduled).
Length: 20.25ft (6.2m).
Range: 300-500nm (556-926.6km).
Guidance: active radar homing.
Anti-Ship (T-ASM) and Land Attack (T-LAM, range 2,000nm, 3,700km) versions. Evaluation in *Merrill* (DD 976). To be fitted to major surface units.

Harpoon (RBM-84)

In service: 1977.
Length: 15ft (4.6m).
Range: 60nm (111km).
Guidance: active radar homing.
Fired from lightweight canisters fixed to quadruple ramps on CGs and latest DDs, and from a variety of launchers (Mk 11, Mk 13, Mk 16 and Mk 26) in other ships. LAMPS helicopter provides relay beyond horizon range.

5-inch/54 cal. Mk 45 (single)

In service: 1974.
Fire Control: SPG-60, SPQ-9 with Mk 86 GFCS.
Lightweight D-P gun with modest performance but good reliability and low manning requirements.

5-inch/54 cal. Mk 42 (single)

In service: 1953.
Fire Control: SPG-53 with Mk 68 GFCS.
High-performance D-P gun. Complex and not always reliable.

76 mm/62 cal. Mk 75 (single)

In service: 1977.
Fire Control: Mk 92 GFCS.
Lightweight high-performance gun manufactured under licence from OTO-Melara for FFG-7 and PHM.

3-inch/50 cal. Mk 33 (twin)

In service: 1944.
Fire Control: Mk 35 radar with Mk 56 GFCS.
Being removed from older CGs and DDs because of maintenance problems but still fitted in some amphibious vessels and auxiliaries. Later installations have aluminium or GRP gun-shield.

20 mm/76 cal. Mk 15 (6 barrels)

In service: 1980.
Fire Control: Local radar.
Phalanx Close-In Weapon System (CIWS). 3,000rpm. To be fitted as standard "last-ditch" anti-missile weapon in 250 warships. Three to be fitted in CVs, two in all other major surface units, including amphibious vessels.

Top right: The first launch of an air-launched AGM-109 Tomahawk missile from an A-6 Intruder in 1976. Similar ship-launched variants are to be fitted to major surface units.

Centre: A 5-inch/54 cal. Mk 42 aboard the frigate *Lockwood* (FF-1064). Modifications have been made to improve the reliability of the gun, which has proved fragile in operation.

Right: Two twin 3-inch/50 cal. guns aboard an auxiliary vessel. Some installations have an aluminium or GRP gunshield.

159

OTHER SUPER-VALUE MILITARY GUIDES IN THIS SERIES......

PRINTED IN BELGIUM BY

INTERNATIONAL BOOK PRODUCTION